In Those Days

In Those Days

Collected Writings on Arctic History

Book 4
Shamans, Spirits, and Faith in the Inuit North

by KENN HARPER

INHABIT
MEDIA

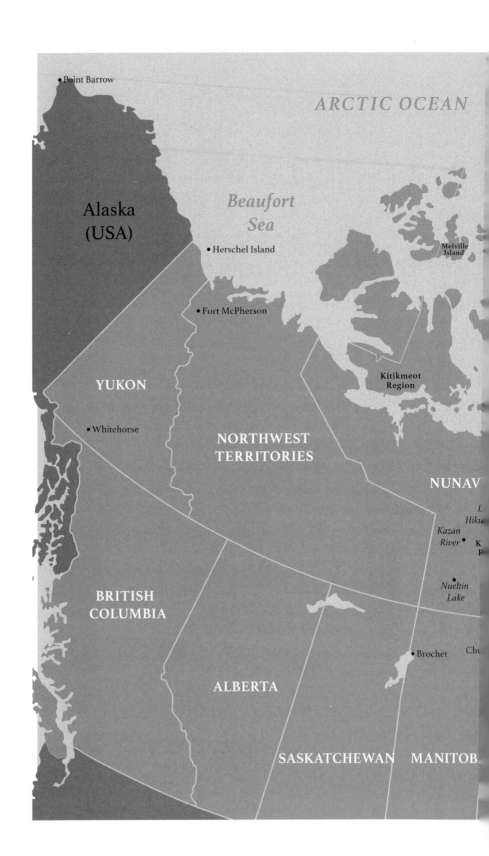

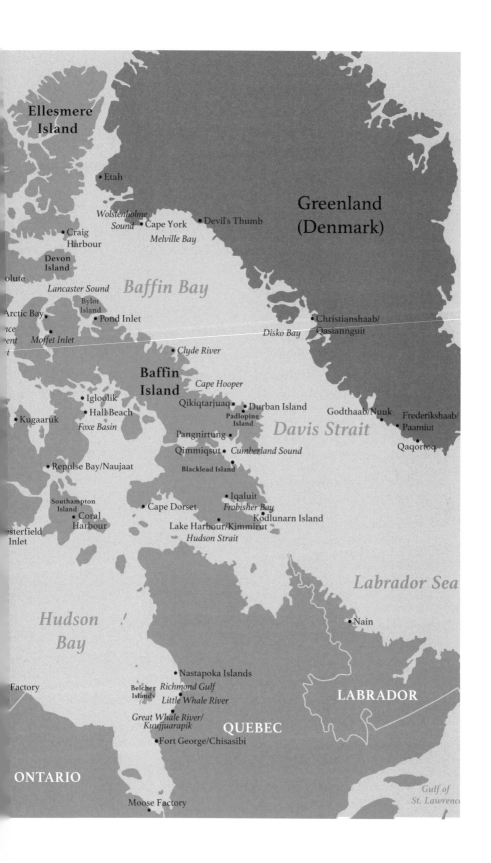

Published by Inhabit Media Inc.
www.inhabitmedia.com

Inhabit Media Inc. (Iqaluit) P.O. Box 11125, Iqaluit, Nunavut, X0A 1H0
(Toronto) 191 Eglinton Avenue East, Suite 310, Toronto, Ontario, M4P 1K1

This project was made possible in part by the Government of Canada.

We acknowledge the support of the Canada Council for the Arts for our publishing
program.

Printed in Canada.

Library and Archives Canada Cataloguing in Publication

Title: Shamans, spirits, and faith in the Inuit North / by Kenn Harper.
Names: Harper, Kenn, author.
Description: Series statement: In those days : collected writings on Arctic history ;
book 4
Identifiers: Canadiana 20190144858 | ISBN 9781772272543 (softcover)
Subjects: LCSH: Inuit—Religion—Anecdotes. | LCSH: Canada, Northern—
Religion—Anecdotes. | LCSH:
    Christianity—Canada, Northern—Anecdotes. | LCSH: Canada, Northern—
History—Anecdotes.
Classification: LCC E99.E7 H37 2019 | DDC 204/.408997120719—dc23

Table of Contents

Introduction   /1
A Note on Word Choice   /5
Preface   /7

Collected Writings
Sedna, the Woman at the Bottom of the Sea   /11
Wedding at Hvalsey Church   /14
The First Thanksgiving in North America   /18
Greenland Language Pioneers   /22
Mikak and the Moravian Church in Labrador   /33
Taboos: Numerous and Irksome Rules of Life   /39
Erasmus Augustine Kallihirua: Inuit Theology Student   /47
The Moravian Mission to Cumberland Sound   /51
The First Inuktitut Language Conference   /60
Father Gasté's Remarkable Journey   /64
Simon Gibbons: First Inuit Minister   /68
Joseph Lofthouse's Wedding Dilemma   /72
Taboos about Animals   /75
Edmund Peck: Missionary to the Inuit   /86
The Blacklead Island Mission   /91
Becoming a Shaman   /111
Isaac Stringer: The Bishop Who Ate His Boots   /132

A Church for Lake Harbour /136

Percy Broughton: The Unknown Missionary /139

Father Turquetil: First Roman Catholic Bishop of
  the Arctic /147

Missionary Names in Cumberland Sound /151

Rules of Life and Death /154

"Coming Up Jesusy" /159

The Spread of Syllabics /170

Orpingalik: "All My Being Is Song" /174

The Power of Magic Words /179

Mercy Flight to Arctic Bay /183

Operation Canon: John Turner's Tragedy at
  Moffet Inlet /187

"And the Stars Shall Fall from Heaven": The Belcher
  Island Murders /194

Donald Whitbread: Learning Inuktitut the Old Way /202

A Well-Travelled Inuktitut Bible /206

Acknowledgements /210

Introduction

This is the fourth volume to result from a series of articles that I wrote over a decade and a half under the title Taissumani for the Northern newspaper *Nunatsiaq News*. This volume presents beliefs, traditions, and histories, most of them from the Canadian Arctic and a few from Greenland. They are stories about Inuit, about Qallunaat (white people), and often about the interactions between these two very different cultures. For some chapters there is an extensive paper trail; for others it is scanty. Inuit maintain some of these stories as part of their vibrant oral histories. We need to know these stories for a better understanding of the North today, and the events that made it what it is. They enhance our understanding of Northern people and contribute to our evolving appreciation of our shared history.

I lived in the Arctic for fifty years. My career has been varied; I've been a teacher, businessman, consultant, and municipal affairs officer. I moved to the Arctic as a young man and worked for many

In Those Days

years in small communities in the Qikiqtaaluk (then Baffin) region—one village where I lived had a population of only thirty-four. I also lived for two years in Qaanaaq, a community of five hundred in the remotest part of northern Greenland. Wherever I went, and whatever the job, I immersed myself in Inuktitut, the language of Inuit.

In those wonderful days before television became a staple of Northern life, I visited the elders of the communities. I listened to their stories, talked with them, and heard their perspectives on a way of life that was quickly passing.

I was also a voracious reader on all subjects Northern, and learned the standard histories of the Arctic from the usual sources. But I also sought out the lesser-known books and articles that informed me about Northern people and their stories. In the process I became an avid book collector and writer.

All the stories collected in this volume originally appeared in my column, Taissumani, in *Nunatsiaq News*. *Taissumani* means "long ago." In colloquial English it might be glossed as "in those days," which is the title of this series. The columns appeared online as well as in the print edition of the paper. Because of this, it came as a surprise to me to learn that I had an international readership. I know this because of the comments that readers sent me. I say it was a surprise because I initially thought of the columns as being stories for Northerners. No one was writing popular history for a Northern audience, be it Indigenous or non-Indigenous. I had decided that I would write stories that would appeal to, and inform, Northern people. Because of where I have lived and learned, and my knowledge of Inuktitut, these stories would usually (but not always) be about the Inuit North. The fact that readers elsewhere in the world show an interest in these stories is not only personally gratifying to me, but should be satisfying to

Northerners as well—the world is interested in the Arctic.

I began writing the series in January of 2005, and temporarily ended it in January of 2015. I began it again in 2018. I write about events, people, or places that relate to Arctic history. Most of the stories—for that is what they are, and I am simply a storyteller—deal with northern Canada, but some are set elsewhere in the Arctic. My definition of the Arctic is loose—it is meant to include, in most of the geographical scope of the articles, the areas where Inuit live, and so this includes the sub-Arctic. Sometimes I stray a little even from those boundaries. I don't like restrictions, and *Nunatsiaq News* has given me free rein to write about what I think will interest its readers.

The stories are presented here substantially as they originally appeared in Taissumani, with the following cautions. Some stories which were presented in two or more parts in the original have been presented here as single stories. For some, the titles have been changed. There have been minimal changes and occasional corrections to text. I have occasionally changed punctuation in direct quotations, if changing it to a more modern and expected style results in greater clarity.

The chapters have been organized in more or less chronological order, but they have not been presented as a section on traditional beliefs followed by a section on Qallunaat missionary activity. I wanted to integrate traditional beliefs with Christian beliefs and show the transition from one to the other. The chapters are meant to be read independently.

Qujannamiik.
Kenn Harper
Ottawa, Canada

A Note on Word Choice

nuk is a singular noun. It means, in a general sense, a person. In a specific sense, it also means one person of the group we know as Inuit, the people referred to historically as Eskimos. The plural form is *Inuit*.

A convention, which I follow, is developing that *Inuit* is the adjectival form, whether the modified noun is singular or plural; thus, an Inuit house, Inuit customs, an Inuit man, Inuit hunters.

The language spoken by Inuit in Canada is Inuktitut. In Nunavut in recent years, the overall term for the language has become Inuktut, with Inuktitut being used to designate the dialects of the eastern and east-central Arctic, and Inuinnaqtun used to describe the dialect spoken in the western Kitikmeot region. That spoken in Labrador is called Inuttut. Greenlanders call their language Kalaallisut.

The word *Eskimo* is not generally used today in Canada, although it is commonly used in Alaska. I use it if it is appropriate

In Those Days

Aua explained, "The greatest peril of life lies in the fact that human food consists entirely of souls." Inuit feared the souls of the animals on whom their lives depended, along with the souls of dead human beings.

The number of taboos—*pittailiniit*—proliferated as society and human interactions became more complex. For some groups, adherence to them was quite onerous. Many of them are detailed in the chapters that follow.

Into this harsh yet beautiful world came uninvited strangers—Qallunaat, non-Inuit. Explorers, whalers, and traders. Most explorers were little interested in the Inuit they encountered. If they bothered with them at all, it was to employ them as guides to help them in their quest for far-off lands and resources. The whalers were more involved. They employed Inuit hunters as boatmen, and women as seamstresses; they also bought products that Inuit themselves had taken from the land and sea. The traders were more engaged with Inuit than were the explorers or whalers. Traders were there not to hunt or fish themselves, but to encourage the Inuit in those pursuits and to trade—often at exorbitant exchange rates—for furs, ivory, and oil.

A fourth group of Qallunaat were usually, but not always, the last to arrive in Inuit Nunangat—the land of the Inuit. These men, for they were all men (although some were accompanied by their wives), did not hunt or fish commercially, nor were they in quest of new lands. With some exceptions, they didn't trade. They had a more esoteric goal, for they were interested in the souls of the Inuit. These were the missionaries.

Their message was difficult to understand. It was written in books, but the Inuit lacked literacy. And so, over time, the missionaries learned the language of the Inuit, wrote down their words, and created written forms that they could teach to the Inuit so that they could read and write words themselves. The Qallunaat pioneers in Inuit language learning were early missionaries active in Greenland. Later missionaries in northern Canada followed their examples. Some of their stories are recounted in this volume.

The missionaries sought to eradicate the traditional beliefs of the Inuit. Most Inuit took quickly to the new religion, as a means of release from the observance of the stifling taboos. The new beliefs spread quickly, as did the ability to read and write. In the eastern Canadian Arctic, the Syllabic writing system was learned so quickly that literacy spread well in advance of missionary travel. The ministers and priests distributed books in the new script, which made their way to isolated camps. But understanding of what was written was not so easily acquired. In some areas, confused versions of the Christian message led to misunderstandings and occasionally to deaths. In some places, men set themselves up as prophets—or as God himself—with unexpected or tragic consequences.

In northern Baffin Island and down the west coast of Foxe Basin as far as Repulse Bay (now Naujaat), a curious ritual developed under the very noses of the recently arrived traders; if their scant written records can be believed, they didn't notice. This was the ritual of *siqqitirniq*. It centred around food—the focus of many taboos—and it sought to integrate certain features of Christianity into the Inuit belief system, while freeing Inuit from the necessity to follow the taboos. The practice of *siqqitirniq* is explained in the chapters that follow.

In some geographic areas, such as Labrador, where the Moravians held sway, the missionaries had no competition. Elsewhere, there were rival denominations—Roman Catholics and Anglicans in the early years in Canada. Inuit were accustomed to rivalries between shamans and tolerated the competition between priests and ministers, even if they did not fully comprehend the subtle differences in their messages. Eventually some Inuit converts themselves became catechists and ministers of the gospel.

The chapters that follow document Inuit traditional beliefs as well as telling the stories of the missionaries, and their converts, who brought a different message to the Inuit.

Sedna, the Woman at the Bottom of the Sea

I have sometimes been asked about the word *Sedna*, which is often used in books on Inuit art and legend. Carvings of the being known as Sedna are popular, and the name has found many usages in popular culture.

Sedna is one of many names that refer to a creature from mythology, a woman who lives at the bottom of the sea and who sometimes withholds the bounty of the harvest from Inuit hunters.

There are a number of versions of the story. In one, a young woman was visited by a handsome stranger and took him as her husband. He was revealed to be a dog in human form, and left the woman pregnant. Her father, ashamed, banished her to an island, where she gave birth to a number of children whom she set adrift on kamik soles—these became the ancestors of Qallunaat and

In Those Days

First Nations people. Her father eventually travelled to the island to take his daughter home. But a storm arose and, fearing the boat would capsize, he threw her overboard to lighten the load. As she clung to the boat, he cut off her fingers—these became seals, walruses, and whales, the bounty of the sea. The girl sank to the sea floor, where she became Sedna and controlled hunters' access to the sea mammals on which they depended.

In times of famine it was necessary for an *angakkuq*—a shaman—to make a dangerous trip to Sedna's home to arrange for the release of the animals so that hunters might have success in their hunt.

Some of her other names in various geographical regions are Nuliajuk, Taliilajuq, Nerrivik, Uinigumasuittuq ("the one who does not want to marry"), and Takannaaluk Arnaaluk ("the terrible woman down there").

In southern Baffin Island, the name "Sanna" is used. It is this name that has been popularized with the spelling "Sedna."

The earliest written reference to this name is in the diary of Brother Mathias Warmow, a German Moravian missionary from Greenland who spent a winter in Cumberland Sound in the 1850s and recorded the name as "Sanak" or "Sana."

Charles Francis Hall, who explored Frobisher Bay in the early 1860s and whose spelling of Inuit names was usually very inexact, called her "Sidne," and on his second voyage, "Sydney"!

The spelling that has become so popular, Sedna, is that of Franz Boas, the pioneer anthropologist who spent the winter of 1883–84 in Cumberland Sound and wrote the first major ethnological work on Canadian Inuit, *The Central Eskimo*. Boas wrote a great deal about Inuit belief in "Sedna." His spelling may not even be so far off the mark, for the name may once have been "Satna"—there has been a tendency in recent years in Baffin towards the gemination of consonant clusters. Remember also that it is only in the last few decades that Inuktitut spelling has been standardized in either Syllabic or Roman orthography.

I have often also wondered if the name is not, in fact, merely a demonstrative pronoun, used, as was often the case in Inuktitut, to avoid using a proper name, especially of one fearful or deserving of respect. The name used in Iglulik, "Takannaaluk Arnaaluk"—"the terrible woman down there"—is built on this model, and the first word of it is derived from *kanna*—"the one down there." Could not "Sanna" be simply a variant of this? (Schneider's *Ulirnaisigutiit*—a dictionary of Nunavik dialects—records *sanna* as meaning "down there" on the Hudson's Bay coast of Quebec.)

The word has survived into modern times and is used throughout southern Baffin Island. In a Pangnirtung oral history project in about 1986, Qattuuq Evic recounted the times when the Inuit worshipped "a false god who they called Sanah." In an Arctic College publication from 1999, *Transition to Christianity*, Victor Tungilik from Naujaat said, "She has been given different names. She has been called Sanna. In my dialect she is called Nuliajuk. Among the Iglulingmiut, she is called Takannaaluk."

Sedna, the popularized spelling of Sanna, is synonymous with Nuliajuk and the other variants of the name. The words are used in different parts of the Inuit world, but their meaning is the same.

Wedding at Hvalsey Church

One thousand years ago, Greenland was inhabited not by Inuit, but by white men from Iceland and Norway. For almost five hundred years Norsemen lived in southwest Greenland, in colonies that dated from the time of Erik the Red in the year 985. The Norse were farmers and herdsmen, and they had found a land lush with vegetation, mild in the winter. Potatoes and other vegetables grew in the warm summers, and cattle, sheep, goats, and horses thrived. It had been the Norsemen's good fortune to discover Greenland during a mild climatic period.

At its peak, the Norse population probably reached four or five thousand. In the "Eastern Settlement," actually in southern Greenland near present-day Qaqortoq, there were about 190 dwellings, and in the "Western Settlement," five hundred kilometres farther north near present-day Nuuk, were another 90.

The Norse hunted too. They travelled north along the coast at least as far as Upernavik in search of polar bear, walrus, and narwhal. They traded bear skins and ivory tusks to Europe. The narwhal tusk, in particular, was highly prized; it was thought to be the horn of the legendary unicorn, and was worth its weight in gold.

About the year 1250, the ancestors of the present-day Greenlanders entered Greenland by way of Ellesmere Island. These were Inuit of the Thule Culture. They migrated rapidly southward along the coast. The Norse first encountered them on their hunting trips to the north. They called them Skraellings. Within a hundred years of their arrival in Greenland, they had reached the Western Settlement. In fact, by the mid-fourteenth century no Norse were to be found in that settlement. A relief expedition from the Eastern Settlement reported in the 1350s: "Now the Skraellings have the entire Western Settlement; though there are plenty of horses, goats, oxen and sheep, all wild, but no people, Christian or heathen."

During the 1400s, contact between Europe and the Norse in Greenland ceased. In 1721 Hans Egede, a Norwegian missionary, arrived in Greenland in quest of the remnants of the Norse colony. He assumed that they had survived, and his intention was to reconvert them to Christianity. But he found no one there except Inuit.

Egede's son Niels, who learned well the language of the Greenlandic Inuit, heard from a shaman about attacks on the Norse colonies by European pirates. Regarding one attack, Niels Egede wrote, "The surviving Norsemen loaded their vessels with what was left and set sail to the south of the country, leaving some behind, whom the Greenlanders [Inuit] promised to assist if something bad should happen. A year later, the evil pirates returned and, when the Greenlanders saw them, they took flight, taking along some of the Norse women and children, to the fjord, leaving the others in the lurch."

That fall, when the Greenlanders returned, they saw that the houses and farms had been set afire and destroyed. They took the remaining Norse women and children into the fjord with them. "And there," Egede tells us, "they remained in peace for many years, taking the Norse women into marriage."

These reports tell of three causes of the disappearance of the Norse from Greenland. Undoubtedly there were instances of friction between the Norse and the Inuit, and Inuit legends tell of battles between the two sides. There were also attacks by European pirates. No doubt some of the Norse left the country and returned to Europe, or tried to. Others may have tried to escape to North America, their fabled Vinland.

But other causes of their disappearance must also be accepted. Bubonic plague had ravaged Europe in the mid-1300s, ruining its economy. Demand for Greenlandic products declined. The climate had also worsened. A period of severe climate called the Little Ice Age had begun, and the land was no longer conducive to agriculture. The Norse failed to adapt their lifestyle to the deteriorating conditions—they did not learn from their Inuit neighbours how to make their living from the sea. Those who did not leave or were not killed in battle died or intermarried with the Inuit.

The last dated reference to the Norse in Greenland is an account of a wedding at Hvalsey Church near Qaqortoq, in the

Eastern Settlement. The marriage of Sigrid Bjornsdottir and Tor-
stein Olavsson took place on September 16, 1408, officiated by
two priests who had read the banns on three consecutive Sundays.
By this time the colony was in decline. Sporadic references to the
Norse in Greenland continued to appear in Europe from time to
time until eventually the colony was forgotten.

The First Thanksgiving in North America

Before 1957, Thanksgiving in Canada was celebrated at various times; since the First World War it had been observed in November, in the same week as Remembrance Day. On January 31, 1957, Parliament, under Prime Minister Louis St. Laurent, proclaimed the second Monday in October to be "a day of General Thanksgiving to Almighty God for the bountiful harvest with which Canada has been blessed." Thanksgiving has been in October ever since.

The wording of the proclamation reflected the largely rural culture of Canada at the time. Thanking God for the harvest that would sustain them through the winter was a continuation of the tradition begun in Massachusetts in 1621, when the Pilgrims gave thanks for their first harvest. That celebration, it has been noted, was as much a thanks for having survived their arduous voyage to America.

But the Pilgrims were not the first to celebrate, through a formal giving of thanks, in North America. That honour is often given to Sir Martin Frobisher and his crew for celebrating North America's first Thanksgiving in 1578. But that is a mistake, despite what almost every history book and Internet source will tell you. The event happened, but Frobisher did not participate in it. In fact, he wasn't even there.

Frobisher's third voyage, comprising fifteen ships, was a mining venture—a search for the gold that the explorer thought he had found on a previous expedition. But it was also to be a voyage of colonization, for Frobisher was to leave one hundred men in "the land now called Meta Incognita."

The ships crossed the Atlantic in June, with a stop on the Greenland coast. But the mouth of Frobisher Bay was "choked up with ice," to use the words of Frobisher's chronicler, George Best. One ship, the *Dennis*, sank, taking with it part of the prefabricated house, which spelled the end of the colonization scheme. The *Judith* and the *Michael* were separated from the fleet and presumed lost. Frobisher, on the *Ayde*, followed by a number of other ships, entered the turbulent waters of Hudson Strait, which he named "Mistaken Straytes." He thought it might be the entrance to a Northwest Passage and that he could have sailed through it to China, but those were not his orders, and he resumed his course for Frobisher Bay.

The *Judith* and the *Michael*, in the meantime, had not sunk after all, but had separated and experienced heavy ice and storms in trying to enter Frobisher Bay. They were reunited on July 13. Best wrote that "from the night of the first storm, which was about the first day of July, until ... the sixe and twentieth of the same, they never sawe any one day or houre, wherein they were not troubled with continuall daunger and feare of deathe."

On July 20 the *Judith*, under Captain Edward Fenton, finally made anchor in the bay near an island known as Winter's Furnace. Two days later, on Countess of Warwick's Island—now called Kodlunarn Island, a misspelling of the Inuktitut word for "white man"—the crew gave thanks for their deliverance from the savage weather they had endured. The *Judith* carried an Anglican clergyman, the Reverend Robert Wolfall, described as "being of good reputation among the best," a man who was "well seated and settled at home in his own country, with a good and large living, having a good honest woman to wife, and very towardly children."

Wolfall celebrated Holy Communion for the crew, the first such Christian service ever held in what would one day become Canada. They continued that day "in prayer and thanks giving to God, as well for the delivering of us from the dangers past, as also for his great goodness in placing us in so safe an harbour. Desiring him of his mercy to continue this his great good favour towards us."

And so this first celebration of Thanksgiving in North America was not in thanks for a successful harvest, but rather for a safe passage and a safe harbour at their destination. But it was Thanksgiving nonetheless.

Frobisher arrived from Hudson Strait a number of days later, overjoyed to find the crews of the *Judith* and the *Michael* alive. He and his crew knelt and gave "humble and hearty thanks" to God. Then Reverend Wolfall preached a sermon. This too was a service of Thanksgiving, and Holy Communion may have been served. He exhorted the crews "to be thankful to God for their strange and miraculous deliverance in those so dangerous places, and ... willed them to make themselves always ready, as resolute men, to enjoy and accept thankfully whatsoever adventure his divine Providence should appoint."

Greenland Language Pioneers

Poul Egede: The First Translations

Hans Egede, the first missionary to Greenland, arrived there in 1721 in search of the lost Norse colony, and remained to convert the Inuit. He laboured there for fifteen years. He attempted to learn the language of the Greenlanders, but in this he experienced great difficulty. Still, in his best-known book on the country, which in translation would be titled *New Description of Old Greenland*, he gave the first description and systematic outline of the language spoken there. This was, in fact, the first description of any branch of the Eskimo language.

Hans Egede's son Poul was twenty years old when he arrived in Greenland with his family. This was a much better age to begin learning a new language, and he made more rapid progress than his father. He fitted in well with the Greenlanders and eventually became missionary at Christianshaab in Disko Bay.

Poul Egede—Pavia to the Greenlanders—began translating the Bible in January of 1737. Eventually he translated the first three books of Moses. He found that Greenlandic lacked terms for many of the words and concepts he needed to translate, and so he began the practice of using Danish words, which eventually became standardized as part of the language. "Thus began," in the words of Finn Gad, the great historian of Greenland, "the process of evolution in the West Greenlandic language which, starting with the 'church language' gradually came to include the lay language as well."

Egede's job was to bring the Bible to the Greenlanders. He was as meticulous in his translations as it was possible to be, but he continually revised what had already been translated, always in search of the correct word. He employed a Greenlandic woman, Arnarsaaq, to help him in his translations, and his practice of constant revision upset her. She thought the word of God should be unchangeable, and asked Egede why it was permissible to change His words so often. "I do not doubt," she said, "that the Word is true, but those who are not well versed in it might think it is not the truth, since it varies so much."

Poul Egede returned to Europe in 1740, but he continued his involvement with the Greenland mission until his death in 1789. He translated parts of both the Old and New Testaments into Greenlandic. But he is best known (at least outside Greenland) for his dictionary, published in 1750, and his grammar, published ten years later.

A later missionary, Otto Fabricius, wrote this in the preface to his own later Greenlandic grammar:

In Those Days

It is now thirty-one years since the first *Grammatica Gronlandica* saw the light, compiled by the late Bishop Povel [Poul] Egede, my old teacher whom I always loved and honoured as my father and whose memory will ever be sacred to me. All who have considered his work with discernment, as the first of its kind, must with me call it a masterpiece; for writing a grammar of so difficult and unknown a language, in which there were no national writings for guidance and which bears practically no likeness to any of those previously known, was by no means an easy matter. In it everything had to be taken up from the beginning, the rules thought out, established and arranged for the first time—and all this by a man who himself had not learnt the language according to rules but solely by practising in daily intercourse with the Greenlanders. And who may not then admire that the work succeeded so well?[1]

Otto Fabricius: Translator and Scholar

Otto Fabricius was born in Denmark on March 13, 1744, the son of a clergyman who was a friend of Hans Egede, the first missionary to Greenland. Greenland was often a topic of conversation at the vicarage where Fabricius grew up, where Hans Egede was a frequent visitor. Otto's older half-brother had been a missionary to Greenland for a short time, returning home when Otto was twenty.

---

[1] Erik Holtved, Otto Fabricius's *Ethnographical Works, Meddelelser om Grønland*, Vol. 140, No. 2 (Copenhagen: C. A. Reitzels Forlag, 1960), 12.

Educated largely at home, Fabricius graduated in 1762 with honours in geometry, arithmetic, and astronomy. Of course, he also studied theology, as well as oriental languages. He attended the Seminarium Groenlandicum, founded by Hans Egede, where Bishop Poul Egede was professor of Greenlandic after his return from Greenland.

At the age of twenty-four Fabricius went out as a missionary of the Lutheran Church to Frederikshaab on the west Greenland coast. For the first three years, he had a room in the collective bunkhouse built for the Danes living there, but increasingly he wanted to be among the Greenlanders.

In the summer of 1770 he made what was, for a missionary at that time, a major move. He left the colony and moved thirty kilometres south, to a spot called Iluilarssuk—it means "the lovely peninsula"—and moved into a spacious "Greenlander house," a house of stones, turf, and timber, that stood high above a small lake. He lived there for three years, living as the Inuit did. He wore skin clothing and learned to hunt seal from a kayak as his friends, the hunters, did. Indeed, it was his seal-hunting costume that gave rise to his Greenlandic name, Erisaalik—"the one in the water-proof kayak-dress," a reference to the distinctive costume that the hunter wore when at sea in his kayak.

Fabricius believed that the Inuit became destitute when confined to the restricted environment of the trading station, and he encouraged their dispersal along the coast to have better access to seal hunting.

He had begun to learn Greenlandic even before he left Denmark and had of course made considerable progress in mastering the language during his three years at the Frederikshaab colony. But once he had moved out of the colony, as the only white man at his remote location, Fabricius's facility with the language increased rapidly. He hunted, and he talked of hunting and community life with his neighbours. Each day he gained in experience and knowledge and recorded what he had learned in the privacy of his hut. It was a busy life. "My sojourn at Iluilarssuk gave me more to do than ever before," he wrote.

Fabricius's health suffered as a result of the hardships of his chosen life. The idyll lasted only three years before he had to bid farewell to his beloved Greenlanders and return, against his will, to Denmark. His total time in Greenland was only six years.

He continued to study and research, first in Norway and then in Denmark proper. His famous work *Fauna Groenlandica* was completed in Norway and published in 1780. That same year he was elected a member of the Danish Academy of Sciences and Letters. He became lecturer in Greenlandic (replacing Poul Egede) in 1789.

A portrait of Fabricius shows a dour, stern-looking man. But he was a man with an enthusiastic passion for research. He was orthodox and conservative when it came to religion, and remained, for the rest of his life, a staunch and stubborn defender of the interests of the Greenlanders. He, unlike most other missionaries, had lived alone among the Greenlanders, observed their customs intimately, and documented their language systematically.

Otto Fabricius made his mark on scientific scholarship of the late 1700s and early 1800s with his publications on the zoology, ethnography, and language of Greenland.

He built, of course, on the earlier work of his friend Poul Egede. His works, in retrospect, share some of the faults found in his friend's works. Like Egede, Fabricius did not distinguish the uvular from the velar consonants—in simple terms, he did not hear, or at least did not record, the difference between the letters *q* and *k*. This was unfortunate. As any student of Inuit languages knows, this is the most significant difference in the language, and that difference is important in determining meaning in many words.

In addition, he showed no interest in recording dialectal differences. He made no musings in what one would today call comparative philology. Indeed, he confined his language writings to the one language that he studied—West Greenlandic. This was the language he needed for his own missionary work, to teach young Greenlanders and later to teach young missionaries who would follow his example by going to Greenland to teach the Inuit.

Fabricius carried the study of Greenlandic well past the work of Egede. His grammar has been described as "not speculative but faithful and methodical in description, a work of the age of Rationalism." In attempting to describe the complex grammar of the language, he wrote that "there are so many forms in the various examples that even those who should best understand the Greenlandic language run the risk of making mistakes in it." Yet as one of the great scholar's biographers, Erik Holtved— a man whom it was my pleasure to meet a number of decades ago, when I was quite new to Arctic studies—observed, "It is undeniably very complicated, and yet every Eskimo can speak his language and do so faultlessly."

Fabricius's language work falls into two categories. The first comprises translations of the Bible, catechisms, hymns, other church works, and textbooks into Greenlandic. The second comprises descriptions of the language.

His translations were independent works, rather than revisions of the earlier works of Egede. For this he faced bitter criticism from older theologians, and especially from H. C. Glahn,

In Those Days

a professor of Greenlandic, who happened to be Poul Egede's son-in-law. Glahn felt that Fabricius was "scrapping" the work of Egede, and he resented the fact that a man who had spent only six years in Greenland would do so. In a perverse echo of Sir Isaac Newton's famous phrase, "If I have seen further, it is by standing on the shoulders of giants," Glahn wrote viciously against Fabricius, "If dwarfs would seek to hop upon the giant's tomb, that would be intolerable to the department." Yet it was Fabricius who completed the unfinished work of Poul Egede, the complete translation of the Bible.

Fabricius would not relent, but he compromised to some extent by agreeing that in the preface to his work Egede would be given due credit. Erik Holtved felt that "by its clarity and true style his Greenlandic translation signified a great advance."

Fabricius made two major contributions to the description of the Greenlandic language. In 1791 he published a grammar of Greenlandic, which was an improvement on the earlier grammar of Egede. This volume is extremely scarce, as most copies of it, still undistributed, were destroyed in a warehouse fire in Copenhagen in 1795. The volume was reprinted in 1801. Even this volume is quite scarce today.

Like Egede, Fabricius also compiled a Greenlandic-Danish dictionary. Published in 1804, *Den Gronlandske Ordbog*, at 795 pages, was more than double the size of Egede's dictionary of fifty-four years earlier. It remained a standard for many years.

Otto Fabricius died in 1822. On his deathbed, he lay correcting the proofs of his Greenlandic translation of the book of Genesis, devoted to his work for the Inuit to the end.

Why should today's young students of Inuktitut and Greenlandic care about the works of old white men like Poul Egede and Otto Fabricius? They should care especially about the dictionaries these men compiled. In them are found many words that have passed out of existence, archaic words that show the richness of the Inuit languages. Perhaps young Indigenous scholars might someday rehabilitate some of these forgotten words and use them to revitalize dialects that continue to face pressure from other languages in a rapidly modernizing world.

Samuel Kleinschmidt: Orthographic Pioneer

Samuel Kleinschmidt was a most remarkable man. He lived at a time and place that ideally suited him to carry on the earlier Greenlandic language work of Poul Egede and Otto Fabricius. Moreover, he was a writer, printer, cartographer, scientist, sociologist, and missionary, as well as a linguistic genius.

Saamuali, as the Greenlanders called him, was born to a German father, the Moravian missionary Johan Conrad Kleinschmidt, and a Danish mother in 1814 at the mission station of Lichtenau in southern Greenland. He spent his early childhood there and grew up speaking Greenlandic.

At the age of nine, he was sent to school in Germany, and from there eventually to Holland to work as a chemist's assistant. For four years he taught at a Moravian mission centre in Denmark. Then in 1840, at the age of twenty-six, he returned to Greenland to take up his life's work.

He was posted to the Moravians' New Herrnhut mission near Godthaab (now Nuuk). He immediately set to work to update his knowledge of Greenlandic. He wanted to know the language and culture intimately, and so he spent most of his time with the Greenlanders. Soon he was able to teach in faultless Greenlandic. He preached without manuscript, and his sermons have been described as "informal yet substantial."

Kleinschmidt knew languages—Greenlandic, Danish, German, English, French, Latin, Greek, and Hebrew. His study of Greenlandic quickly led him to believe that the orthography then in use for Greenlandic was inadequate and inconsistent. He set out to correct it. In 1851, his definitive grammar of Greenlandic was published in Berlin. It remained the cornerstone of Greenlandic language study for over a century. The University of Berlin eventually offered him a doctorate for this work, but Kleinschmidt turned it down, saying, "One has no use for that sort of thing in Greenland."

In 1856 the community of Zeist, where he had lived in Holland, sent Kleinschmidt a printing press. Heinrich Rink, the governor, acquired one the following year. Godthaab became an Arctic hotbed of intellectual activity. Rink's press issued its first publication in 1857, Kleinschmidt's the following year.

Kleinschmidt's first book was *Nunalerutit*, meaning simply *A Geography*. It bore the subtitle *A Primer on the Nature of the World and its Inhabitants*. It was sixty pages in length and designed to bring some knowledge of the rest of the world to the Greenlanders. So was his second volume, a world history, published the following year. These accomplishments are all the more impressive when one realizes that Kleinschmidt had never seen a printing press before 1856. Yet his books show "refinement and elegance." He was not only printer, but also binder and distributor.

In 1859 Kleinschmidt had a falling-out with the Moravian Church over matters of church discipline and educational methods. He was summoned to Germany to explain himself but refused to go. "In Greenland I am and in Greenland I stay," he replied. He left the Moravian community and moved to nearby Godthaab, entering the Danish educational establishment. He took his printing press with him and continued to write and publish prolifically.

Among his books was an 1863 publication about animals of the world, in which Kleinschmidt had to create names for foreign animals, names still used today. He called the elephant, in reference to its stiff-legged gait, "the one which has no joints." One book, *Tales about the Missionaries*, contained a map of the world so large that it had to be folded several times to fit within the covers, like a modern road map. The book went through two editions, totalling sixteen hundred copies. The map was too large to be printed on his press, and so, amazingly, Kleinschmidt drew each of the sixteen hundred maps himself, and coloured each in watercolour.

Near the end of his life, Kleinschmidt wrote a curious sixteen-page pamphlet. Called *About those who are working for a revolution*, it was a diatribe against the socialist movement in Europe. He was an extremely conservative man living in a conservative community. The pamphlet expressed his horror and fear of socialism, which he saw as "The Beast" in St. John's Revelations. The book is now extremely rare.

Kleinschmidt's dream was to retranslate the entire Bible into Greenlandic. He succeeded in translating and printing the Old Testament and had nearly completed translating the New Testament by the time of his death.

In Godthaab, Kleinschmidt lived in a one-room Greenlandic-style house with peat walls. Here he wrote—often under a magnifying glass to save paper. An eccentric man, he seldom washed, always wore Greenlandic clothes, and—for some reason biographers like to mention this—he never wore underwear. The king awarded him a gold medal of merit, but he never wore it. "One has no wish for a gold medal on an anorak," he said. He refused a visit from a visiting prince with the words, "One has no time." A bachelor, he nonetheless loved children and spoke to them only in Greenlandic.

A man ahead of his time, Samuel Kleinschmidt laid the foundation for modern Greenlandic studies. He died on February 9, 1886. Interred in the Moravian cemetery, his remains were moved to Godthaab in 1907, where they lie behind the historic Lutheran church at the harbour.

Mikak and the Moravian Church in Labrador

Mikak was the most well-travelled Inuk of her time. She was born on the Labrador coast about 1740, but we know nothing of her life until she was twenty-five. In the summer of 1765 she met the Moravian missionaries Jens Haven and Christian Drachart in Chateau Bay, in far southern Labrador. They were travelling with Hugh Palliser, Governor of Newfoundland and Labrador. He was concerned about the situation of the Inuit in the area near the Strait of Belle Isle, where they had fought with European—English and French—and New England fishermen and sealers for at least the previous fifty years. The Treaty of Paris had been signed in 1763 and led to a reduction in the French presence in the area, but still Palliser hoped to find a way to remove the Inuit from Labrador's south coast and have them return to what he thought were their more traditional lands north of Hamilton Inlet.

Mikak had a husband at the time, but his name is unknown to history. She met the Moravian missionaries in Chateau Bay because bad weather forced them to stay longer than expected; they lived in the tent of Segullia, the brother of Tuglavina, who eventually became Mikak's second husband. She was pleased to discover that both missionaries spoke her language, having learned it in Greenland.

The Moravian Church is an evangelical sect bearing the official name of Unitas Fratrum. One of the oldest Protestant denominations in the world, it traces its roots to the Bohemian Reformation in the fifteenth century, even before the Protestant Reformation. It had missionary efforts throughout the world, including among the Inuit of Labrador and Greenland, and eventually Alaska. Its first attempt at establishing a mission in Labrador, in 1751, ended in tragedy when Johann Christian Erhardt and six companions were killed by Inuit. In 1764 Jens Haven led an exploratory summer voyage to Labrador; he returned the following year when he met Mikak and other Inuit.

In 1767 Francis Lucas, second in command of a garrison at Chateau Bay, captured three Inuit women and six children in an altercation in which as many as twenty Inuit were killed. It is probable that Mikak's husband was among the dead. Lucas kept his captives at York Fort in Chateau Bay for the winter and took them to St. John's the following summer. Later that year, Governor Palliser arranged for Lucas to take three of them to England; these were Mikak, her six-year-old son, Tutauk, and a thirteen-year-old orphan boy, Karpik.

In England Mikak was introduced to Augusta, the dowager

princess of Wales, who presented her with gifts that included a finely ornamented white dress trimmed with gold. A well-known artist, John Russell, painted her portrait. While in England, Mikak met Jens Haven again; he was there petitioning the British government for permission to establish a mission in Labrador, and Mikak strongly encouraged this.

She and her son returned to Labrador in 1769; they were not the first Inuit to travel from Labrador to Europe, but they were the first to ever return.

The stories she told of her experiences in England enhanced her status among her own people, and she used her influence to support the idea of a Moravian mission. By the time Haven and Drachart returned in 1770, she had paved the way for them.

In July of that year, the missionaries met a group at Byron Bay that included Mikak's father, Nerkingoak; he told them that he had renamed his daughter Nutarrak, meaning—as he explained—"changed or new born," because she was so different on her return from Europe. Mikak arrived the next day, wearing her prized possession, the "rich Esquimaux Habit which the Princess Dowager of Wales got made for her in London of fine White Cloth laced with Gold and embroidered with many gold Stars & a Golden Medal of the King hanging at her Breast." Jens Haven noted that "Mikack now Nutarrak ... appears as a great Lady" among her people.

The missionaries expressed some concern for their safety among the Inuit, who had a reputation for fierce behaviour farther south on the coast. Mikak chastised them for these thoughts and assured them that her people would welcome and accept them. "You will see," she said, "how well we will behave, if you will only come. We will love you as our countrymen, and trade with you justly, and treat you kindly." The Moravians returned permanently the following year and established a mission and trading station at Nain.

* * *

The first Moravian convert in Labrador was Kingminguse, who was baptized as Peter in February of 1776. "I have been an Anga-kok [angakkuq], and used to believe what had been told me by my predecessors," he said, "but now I believe it no longer, and will abandon all evil customs for the future, and will follow the Lord Jesus only.... I am alone like an orphan, and have no broth-ers or sisters, and therefore am the more happy that ye will receive me as your brother." Despite this effusive declaration of faith, the man eventually returned to his traditional ways. An illustration of the difficult task faced by the missionaries—who also controlled the supply of trade goods at their station—is shown by a statement from another man, Aula, who was present at Kingminguse's baptism. He said, "I believe very much, but at present I want a knife."

If the missionaries had expected Mikak to remain the mainstay of their support on the coast, they were disappointed. She refused to live at the mission station, and she and her family traded with other nearby traders.

Jens Haven had observed that "her husband is extremely fond of her and extremely cautious not to leave her alone with the Europeans." But Tuglavina had a mercurial temperament. In April of 1773 he traded Mikak to another man, Pualo, in exchange for Pualo's wife, Nochasok, who happened to be Mikak's sister. A month later, he took Mikak back. The trade was on again in April of the following year, and this time it lasted until fall. In the spring of 1776 he traded Mikak to Pualo once again, and this time she remained with him until his death seven years later.

In 1773 Mikak became further estranged from the Moravians, probably because of a request made by her on-again, off-again husband, Tuglavina, and his brother, Segullia, to travel with her to England. James Hutton, a Moravian leader in England, was incensed at the request. He wrote disparagingly of Mikak's earlier visit to England, referring to "the scandalous life Mikak led," and thought the trip had left her worse off than before, saying, "She is prouder, more wretched and miserable than she was before, less contented with the Station she must however submit to & less fit to enjoy for the future, what other Esquimaux call Enjoyment of Life."

In 1780 Mikak wintered at the Nain mission for the first time. Pualo was baptized, taking the Christian name Abraham. Her son, Tutauk, who some years earlier had begun to call himself Palliser after the former governor, took the baptismal name Jonathan. But Mikak was rejected for baptism. The Moravians believed that Christ had the final say in all matters of importance, and His will was made known through the drawing of lots. There could be nothing more important, in the brethren's estimation, than a person's salvation, and so the decision on a person's readiness for baptism could not be made by a mere mortal minister, but only through lots. When Mikak was rejected, she began to distance herself even more from the Moravians.

Two years later, she and her small family, which also included another son or stepson, moved farther south with a large group of Inuit to trade with English fishermen. When they returned the following year, Pualo asked the Moravians to baptize Mikak so that she would be better received when they returned south, but the missionaries refused; they thought the request to be insincere and that "all his [Pualo's] thoughts are taken up with the Europeans." That summer, they returned south anyway, with a group of about 180 Inuit. Some remained at Chateau Bay for a year, some for longer. When they returned to Nain, it was with tales of wife-stealing, murder, and depravity. Early on, Pualo shot a man, Sirkoak, over his dalliance with Mikak. The man survived. Pualo himself died in the first year at Chateau Bay, probably from an infection.

In the years after Pualo's death, Mikak probably continued to travel often to southern Labrador to trade. She spent brief periods at Nain.

In 1795 she returned to Nain; she was ill. She is reported to have told a missionary, "Ah, I have behaved very bad, and am grieved on that account, but what shall I do! I cannot find Jesus again!" The missionaries ministered to her, but she was not baptized. Ten days after her arrival, on October 1, she died, at about fifty-five years of age. She was buried in Nain.

In 2007 Mikak was designated a person of national historic significance under the Historic Sites and Monuments Act. "A charismatic and resourceful woman," her designation read, she "exemplified Inuit self determination, political ability, and economic control at a time of cultural transition."

Taboos

Numerous and Irksome
Rules of Life

Taboos about Pregnancy

Inuit in northern Baffin Island and the Iglulik area converted to Christianity in the early 1920s, but it would be 1929 before the first missionaries arrived in Pond Inlet. In Cumberland Sound, missionary activity began in the 1890s, and in the Repulse Bay (now Naujaat) area in the 1910s.

Prior to the coming of Christianity, life had been governed by a system of taboos—proscriptions on what kind of behaviour was allowed and what was not. Behaviour that would offend the spirits was to be avoided, as it would surely bring on inclement weather, bad hunting, illness, or death.

Early non-Inuit observers of the lives of the Inuit during these times sometimes commented on the effects of these taboos. To outsiders it seemed that, in a time of rapid cultural change, the list of taboos was proliferating at an alarming rate. Some felt that the observance, rather than the breaking, of this long list of taboos might threaten Inuit survival.

The Greenlandic-Danish ethnologist Knud Rasmussen documented a number of taboos when he lived and travelled among the Inuit of the Repulse Bay and Iglulik areas and the central and western Arctic in the early 1920s. Arriving at the same time as the wholesale conversion to Christianity, Rasmussen had a perfect opportunity to comment on these cultural traits.

In remarking on these rules of life, he noted that angering the spirits can "give rise to suffering and hardship, not only for the person who has offended, but for the whole village. Obligations towards the higher powers are thus not a private matter, but one affecting the entire community." He described the rules as "numerous and irksome," but nonetheless mandatory. The most important ones dealt with times when help was most needed—during pregnancy, at birth, in infancy, at the time of the transition from childhood to adulthood, during sickness, at the hour of death, and, most importantly, while hunting.

Here are some of the taboos he documented. These ones deal with pregnancy:

When a young woman in her first pregnancy feels the life of the child in her body, she must undo her hair and tie it at the back of the neck, so that it hangs down loose from the neckband. She must wear it this way for three days. This gives a speedy delivery.

A pregnant woman must be quick to run out of the house or tent whenever she is called from outside. She will then have an easy delivery.

If she is quick to help others, such as people preparing for a journey, then her child will turn out to be a helpful man or woman.

A pregnant woman must not eat animals shot through the heart.

A pregnant woman must never go outside without her mittens on.

A live bee must be rolled over the back of a pregnant woman and afterwards kept. When she has given birth to her child, this bee should be fastened on top of the head in a hair band, as an amulet to give the child long life.

These rules, odd as they may seem today, were the rules that had to be followed by pregnant women so as not to offend the spirits that rule over the Inuit world.

Taboos about Childbirth

Perhaps even more important than the rules governing pregnancy were the numerous rules that governed childbirth itself. These rules were rigorous and had to be strictly followed. This next set of rules were collected by Knud Rasmussen in the Repulse Bay and Iglulik areas in the early 1920s.

When a woman felt the birth pangs beginning, then a snow hut must be built for her if it was winter, a tent if it was summer. The house or tent was quite small and was used only for the actual birth. It was called *irnivik* or *irnivialuk*.

As long as the woman was in the irnivik, the house could not be added to or repaired, even if damaged by bad weather. Once the child was born, a larger house or tent was set up; it was called *kiniqvik*.

Women must effect their own delivery without help, and they must be alone in the irnivik. Even when the birth was difficult, no

In Those Days

one was allowed to assist. Anyone rendering aid would become impure and subject to the same troublesome year-long taboo as the woman herself. The obligations involved interfered so seriously with domestic duties that the community would not allow any married woman, not even the patient's mother, to incur them. The spirits would be angered at the inability of a woman to manage by herself, or the animals would be offended if a woman aiding another in childbirth should touch a newborn infant not of her own bearing.

If a woman had difficulty in childbirth, a shaman could summon his helping spirits and by their help make matters easier, or utter a magic prayer or magic song to ease the birth.

Before the delivery, a woman must have found either a flint or a piece of white quartzite and sharpened it. This was used to cut the umbilical cord. This knife had to be held in the left hand. The cord was tied round, about half an inch from the navel. If the child was a boy, he must have the stump of the umbilical cord when it fell off, and the little knife, as amulets. They were sewn into his inner jacket on either side of the chest.

A newly born infant had to be cleansed by being wiped all over with the skin of a *saarvaq*, a small snipe (a bird). Water could not be used.

If a newborn infant were sung over while being cleansed for the first time, the child would grow up to make many songs of its own.

If the newborn child was particularly wanted and it was earnestly desired that it would live (it is hard to imagine that this would not be the case), then a magic prayer was sung over it, even before it had suckled at the breast for the first time. This prayer was called *anirnirsiut*, a prayer for the spirit of life.

After birth, the child must be placed naked in the mother's *amaut*. Clothes for an infant must not be made until after it was born.

In naming the child, some deceased person was invoked, and the child's mother uttered that person's name. This was connected with the belief in namesake souls. A child cried for a name, and when the deceased one whose name-soul the child would bear was summoned, care had to be taken that all of the qualities that that soul possessed were communicated to the child. In the example given by Rasmussen, if a child were to be named Ujarak, then his mother would say, *"Ujarak, qai-qai tamarpit,"* which meant, "Ujarak, come here quickly, come here quickly all of you, that is to say, bringing all the characteristics that pertain to you."

These were only some of the rules that surrounded the birth of a child in the dim past before Inuit converted to Christianity. The rules were oppressive and difficult to follow. Yet following them was of the utmost importance.

Taboos after Childbirth

Even more and equally onerous rules governed a mother's behaviour in the period after her child was born.

Here are some that Knud Rasmussen learned from the Iglulik shaman Aua and his wife Orulo.

A whole series of taboos governed the activities of a mother who had just given birth, taboos that were necessary for her to follow to ensure the survival of her child, herself, and indeed of her whole camp.

Among the Iglulik Inuit, a pregnant woman had to give birth in a special snow house or tent, alone, without assistance. After the birth, the mother had to clean herself all over, in winter using snow, in summer with water, and she had to cut away any portions of her clothing that may have become stained with blood. After that she could proceed to the kiniqvik, another special dwelling, where she would have to remain with her child for anywhere from one to three months.

While in the kiniqvik, a woman could receive visitors but was strictly forbidden to go visiting herself. She was regarded as so unclean, so dangerous to her surroundings, that her impurity was supposed to issue forth in an actual, albeit invisible, smoke or vapour, which drove away all game. Should she break the taboo against visiting, all this foul smoke or impurity collected in the form of filth in the hair of the Mother of the Sea Beasts (the spirit known as Nuliajuk, Takannaaluk Arnaaluk, or Sedna), who in disgust shut up all the game, leaving mankind to starve. A woman recently delivered must therefore always have her hood thrown over her head when she went out and must never look round after game.

Rules about eating at this time were particularly important. In the kiniqvik, she must have her own *puugutaq*—wooden tray—from which to drink soup and in which to place the meat she ate. She must also have her own cooking pot and her particular wooden ladle, which was used either for soup or for water, and these must always be placed in front of her, near the lamp, the wooden ladle in the wooden mug along with a meat fork made of caribou horn or a piece of pointed marrow bone.

Every morning the woman had to melt ice or snow for drinking water. And each time she drank, she had to put a drop of water into the child's mouth with her middle finger. This must be done immediately after the child was born and repeated every time the mother drank. The middle finger possessed a special power with regard to infants, so that the water dripping into the mouth was thought to prevent the child from ever suffering from thirst. This was especially important for male children, who, in those days, were all destined to be hunters. Among the Inuit, thirst was regarded as the worst of all sufferings, far more dreaded than hunger.

The mother had to have a small skin bag hanging beside her lamp. Whenever she was about to eat, she had to cut off a small piece of meat, rub it on the child's mouth, and place it in the bag before she started eating. This act, called *minguliqtirijuq*, protected the child against hunger and, if the child was a boy, made him skilful in hunting later, bringing an abundance of meat to his home. Another interpretation of that taboo was that it ensured that the soul of the deceased person after whom the child was named would have something to eat.

The new mother was not allowed to cut up meat herself for boiling. This must be done by young girls or older women. She could not take any meat from the pot and place it on her dish until it was cooked. She must take great care not to spill any. If a piece of meat should fall from her dish, it had to be picked up immediately and thrown on the right side of the lamp.

When the stay in the kiniqvik was over, the minguliqtirijuq requirement came to an end. If the child was a boy, the mother then had to take the skin bag, which by now was filled with tiny fragments of meat, and carry it to the breathing hole of a seal. She had to throw all the scraps of meat, all of which had been the first meat to touch her son's lips—symbolically being his first flesh food—into the hole. By throwing the meat back into the sea where it had come from, the pieces could become seals again, to be caught again by the boy when he grew up. If the child was a girl, the scraps of meat were simply thrown out on the edge of the beach. The skin bag was flung out onto the ice.

While in the kiniqvik, the woman had to have the skin from the head of a seal spread over her lap as an apron while she ate. Afterwards, if the child was a boy, the apron was laid out on the ice beside a seal's breathing hole.

During this period, the woman was not allowed to eat the meat of animals killed by anyone other than her own husband. But there was an exception. At certain times of year, three specially chosen men were sent out after walrus; meat caught by those men could be eaten freely.

Women during this period of abstinence could also not eat the meat of animals that were killed suddenly. The seals that they ate must, after being harpooned, have come to the surface at least once more to breathe.

If the child was a boy, the woman had to eat twice a day, but she could never eat her fill. If the child was a girl, she had three meals a day. But if the child was a boy and she wanted him to be especially skilful in hunting—one cannot imagine why she would not want this—then she should eat three times a day, but, again, she should never eat until she was full. The reasoning behind this was that the mother's hunger causes the child to be light and therefore swift in hunting; he would catch game while others were heavy and slow at their tasks.

All of these rules had to be observed for the entire period following the child's birth, before the woman returned to her husband's house.

Erasmus Augustine Kallihirua

Inuit Theology Student

A young Inuk from northwestern Greenland is one of the few Inuit of whom a biography was ever published in book form. The book, *Kalli, The Esquimaux Christian*, is a very rare book today, despite the fact that it was published in a number of editions, both in England and the United States.

Kalli was born in the Thule district in about 1832 and given the name Qalaherhuaq—the name means "the big navel." Both he and his biographers spelled the name Kallihirua and abbreviated it to Kalli. Of his family we know little. His father, Qisunnguaq, died when Kalli was a teenager. His mother, whose name may have been Saattoq, survived her husband. Kalli had a twin, two sisters, and a younger brother.

In 1850, when Kalli was in his late teens, Captain Erasmus

47

In Those Days

Ommanney, in command of a Franklin search vessel, the *Assistance*, arrived at Cape York, Greenland, a well-known meeting place for Inuit, whalers, and explorers. Young Kalli went onboard the ship and agreed to travel with Ommanney as his guide. Ommanney wanted to get to the bottom of reports, circulated by a Greenlandic interpreter on another vessel, of the massacre of two ships' crews some years earlier. Kalli guided Ommanney into Wolstenholme Sound, where a British naval supply vessel, the *North Star*, had wintered. Then they returned to Cape York, where Ommanney interviewed the Inuit there, using Kalli as his interpreter.

(A word of caution. Kalli had never seen English-speaking people before the arrival of the *North Star* the previous year. Doubtless he had learned some rudimentary English that winter. But when a nineteenth-century Arctic explorer says "interpreter," he usually means something like "guide-facilitator-interpreter-helper." For Ommanney, Kalli was all of these things.)

The Inuit of Cape York denied any knowledge of the alleged massacre, and the *Assistance* continued on in the search for the missing Franklin expedition. The vessel wintered near Griffith Island in Barrow Strait, near present-day Resolute. That winter Kalli learned the basics of reading and writing from the sergeant of marines. The following summer, Ommanney attempted to reach Cape York to return Kalli home, but his path was blocked by ice, so he proceeded on to England, taking Kalli with him. On reaching England, the young Inuk took the name Erasmus York—Erasmus after Captain Ommanney's first name, and York after Cape York.

Ommanney brought his young Inuk friend to the attention of the Society for the Promotion of Christian Knowledge in London. They conferred with the Admiralty, and Kalli was sent to

St. Augustine's College in Canterbury to train as a missionary. At St. Augustine's he was taught more reading and writing, and given religious education. The warden of the college wrote of him: "We consider him a youth of intelligence and quick observation.... He is fond of writing and succeeds very well. He is very devout at prayers, and attentive to the religious instruction given him. I think he will one day be of essential use to a missionary to some northern region."

While in Canterbury, Kalli also worked for a year and a half, five hours a day, in a tailor's shop, learning that trade. He also assisted Captain John Washington of the Admiralty in revising an "Esquimaux" dictionary for use by Franklin searching expeditions.

On November 27, 1853, the young man was baptized and changed his name yet again, becoming Erasmus Augustine Kallihirua. The following autumn he left for St. John's, Newfoundland, where he was to take further religious training at the Theological Institution. The plan was that he would then accompany the bishop of Newfoundland on a missionary trip to Labrador the following summer.

He enjoyed his winter in St. John's. His English had improved considerably. In January of 1856 he wrote a letter to a friend: "The weather here is very cold; I feel it more than at Cape York. I have begun to skate and find it a very pleasant amusement. There is a lake a little distance from the college, called 'Quidi Vidi,' on which we practise. The Bishop is very kind and good to me. College here is not so large and fine a place as St. Augustine's; nor are there so many students. I hope that all my kind friends at Canterbury are quite well.... I remain, yours affectionately, Kalli."

That summer Kalli caught a chill while swimming, and he died on June 14. His funeral service was conducted in St. Thomas church, and a graveside service was conducted by Rev. J. G. Mountain, principal of the college.

Kalli was the first of the Inughuit of northwestern Greenland to venture into a world outside the Arctic. He proved himself to be resilient and adaptable, and at the same time popular with all he met. His life was cut short by illness at the tender age of about twenty-four. One has to wonder what he would yet have accomplished had he lived.

The Moravian
Mission to
Cumberland Sound

In the Inuit-inhabited areas of Canada, the Moravian Church is associated with Labrador, where it dominated the history and development of the coast north of Hamilton Inlet for over two centuries. Less well known is that church's interest in the Inuit of Baffin Island in the mid-1800s.

After William Penny, with the help of the Inuk Eenoolooapik, found the entrance to Cumberland Sound—which whalers had previously heard of but couldn't find—first Scottish and then American whalers came to the sound in large numbers. Captain Parker, of the vessel *Truelove*, was concerned about the adverse effects on the Inuit of the rapid lifestyle changes introduced by the newcomers. In 1851, he contemplated taking Brother Samuel Kleinschmidt from Greenland to Cumberland Sound. His plan was thwarted, ironically, because his voyage to Baffin Bay was so successful; he took so many whales that he had no time to pick up Kleinschmidt and deliver him to Baffin Island at the end of the season. Had that plan materialized, the histories of both Greenland and the Canadian Arctic might have turned out quite differently; Kleinschmidt was a man totally fluent in Greenlandic and later went on to standardize the writing of that language in an orthography that stood unrevised for over a century. He was instrumental in the founding of the national Greenlandic newspaper, published numerous books in Greenlandic, and tirelessly encouraged Greenlandic literacy and writing. Imagine the possible results had he arrived and stayed in northern Canada and introduced writing in an alphabetic orthography almost half a century before Edmund Peck brought Syllabics to Baffin Island. Imagine too how Greenlandic literary culture might have developed—and possibly suffered—in his absence. But history is not built on "what ifs." Kleinschmidt remained in Greenland.

After American whalers first over-wintered in Cumberland Sound, William Penny, who was fervently anti-American, formed the Royal Arctic Company to pursue whaling and mining in the sound. He also began to encourage the Moravians to send out a missionary from Greenland to attend to the education of the Inuit.

In 1853 Penny left Scotland for Cumberland Sound with three ships under his command. He hoped to establish a colony in the sound and had received authorization from the Moravian Mission Board to pick up a missionary in Greenland to promote "the religious and temporal improvement of the Esquimaux population." He intended to call at Lichtenfels on the Greenland coast to pick up Brother Mathias Warmow, who would remain for the winter with Penny's party to evaluate the condition of the Inuit in the sound. In the autumn of the following year he would travel to Europe by whaling vessel to report his findings to the elders of the church. Bad weather intervened, however, and heavy ice prevented any of Penny's ships from reaching Lichtenfels. Penny went on to Cumberland Sound without Warmow and took ten bowhead whales in a very successful season.

Penny wintered in the sound and returned briefly to Scotland in the summer of 1854. While there, he wrote to the secretary of the Moravian Mission as follows: "During our summer fishing, we were surrounded by about 270 of the Esquimaux, who appeared to be simple, docile creatures, but prone to give way to evil influences. They expressed themselves desirous to have a kind instructor living among them, who would tell them of their great Father in heaven, and teach the young people to read, and I do hope that it may still be possible for you to supply one."

In September Penny left again for Cumberland Sound and again was unable to make land at Lichtenfels. And the following year he once more failed to pick up the ever-patient Warmow. And so Penny changed his approach. He wrote to the Moravians thus: "The Natives are a most intelligent race, and showed themselves very anxious to receive the teacher I told them of. Many have died since the date of my last visit. If God spares my life, and enables me to take another voyage to their coasts, would it not be possible for you, with timely notice, to procure me a Missionary of your Church to accompany me from Aberdeen."

The Moravians accepted this suggestion. By February of 1857 Brother Warmow was in Fulneck in Yorkshire, England, to spend a few months there improving his English. In June he travelled to Aberdeen to await Penny's departure for Cumberland Sound.

In Those Days

The *Lady Franklin* left Scotland on the last day of June 1857. By the 23rd of July the ship was near the coast of Greenland, and on the last day of that month the crew sighted Baffin Island. Warmow wrote, "My feelings at the first sight of the region where I am to reside ... for a year, I cannot describe. The thought occurred to me that I might perhaps find a grave here."

From August 2 until the 13th the ship coasted the south shore of Cumberland Sound, calling at a number of Inuit camps. Warmow was pleased to discover that the Inuit could understand his Greenland dialect with little difficulty. He was less impressed with the physical condition of the people he met. From Naujartalik, he wrote:

> At 4 o'clock, the captain, the doctor, and myself went on shore. Here we met with three Esquimaux women and a child. They were dwelling in a miserable tent, and their condition was so wretched, that it must have excited pity even in the most unfeeling heart. They were delighted to see us. We took them on board with us, and they received some refreshment. In the evening, a man with his wife and child were brought on board. They were also in a most miserable condition. The man was quite blind, and the woman so weak and ill, that she could not walk without assistance, while the poor infant, about nine months old, cried incessantly, not being able to obtain nourishment from the emaciated mother. I was engaged in conversation with them till midnight. The man often squeezed my hand, and there was no end to their kujanermik [thanks]. As they understood me, and I them, very well, we were able to converse with but little difficulty. I soon told them of the intention of my

coming, and was not a little surprised to find how well they understood it.[1]

On August 5 Penny and his crew landed building materials at Nuvujat on the south shore of the sound and hastily erected a building there while Warmow spent his time visiting the Inuit. On August 9, with the house nearly complete, all the crew went ashore, and Warmow officiated at the first church service ever to be held in Cumberland Sound.

Four days later the *Lady Franklin* set sail for the opposite shore of the sound. In Tornait Harbour she found five ships. Further on she encountered two more vessels. Warmow accompanied an Inuk nearly to the end of the fjord where the ship anchored; he described it as "a poor land, inhabited by poor people." On August 21, when he boarded the ship *Alibi*, he found several Inuit living on board. They understood a little English and had been told that a "minister" was coming to instruct them. Accordingly, they called him by that English term, although he would have preferred to be called by his Christian name or its Greenlandic equivalent, Matiuse.

Near the end of October, the *Lady Franklin* anchored for the winter off Kekerten, and Mathias Warmow prepared to spend the winter ministering to the Inuit and conducting what was in effect a feasibility study into whether the Moravians should establish a permanent mission on Baffin Island.

He devoted considerable attention in his journal to the condition of the Inuit, who had become quite dependent on the whalers

---

[1] *Periodical Accounts Relating to the Missions of the Church of the United Brethren* (London: Printed for the Brethren's Society for the Furtherance of the Gospel, Volume 22, 1856–57). 452.

for trade goods. In one entry he wrote, "I am always sorry to see the Esquimaux wearing European clothes, and, in short, imitating the Europeans in all respects. They were undoubtedly better off in their original state, and more likely to be gained for the Kingdom of God. But when they begin to copy our mode of life, they are neither properly Europeans nor Esquimaux, and will speedily die out, in consequence of the change."

The dependence of the Inuit on the whaling industry took them away from their seasonal hunting pursuits. This in turn deprived families of skins for tents and clothing and of caches of food for the winter. In mid-October Warmow noted that seventy-eight Inuit were camped near the ship. By early November many of them were sick. "This was indeed no wonder," the missionary wrote. "Many were still living in tents, only one skin thick, and usually by no means free from holes. Others had snow-houses, which were undoubtedly better, but still cold enough. They therefore remained on board the ship as much as possible, where, owing to the number crowded together, the heat not unfrequently became very great. This caused perspiration, and when they returned in the evening to their freezing abodes, severe colds were inevitable."

By May the Inuit population at Kekerten had increased to 150, almost half of what Warmow estimated as the population of the entire sound. All were dependent on whaling. But, despite the numbers, there was little opportunity for mission work; most of the Inuit were totally involved in the various aspects of floe-edge whaling and preparing for the imminent summer thaw. There was a downside to this. In order to serve the whalers, they paid little attention to hunting. Warmow wrote: "The Esquimaux were very unfavourably situated at this season, as the sun shone with so much power, as to thaw their snow-houses. Very few had tents, or the skins for constructing them, as they had entirely neglected the pursuit of seals."

In this period of early contact with non-natives, the Inuit seem to have been so impressed with the technology and accomplishments of Europeans that they were willing to attribute almost any feat to the white man. Warmow spoke to them about the creation story: "In conversation with the natives, I referred to the creation of the world. They said that some one must undoubtedly have made all things, but who it was, they did not know. They thought, however, that it must have been a very powerful and clever man, and most likely a European."

On June 25 the ice between ship and shore broke up and was carried away by a strong northeasterly wind. The ship remained for another three weeks. Then on July 19 the *Lady Franklin* finally left the harbour at Kekerten that had been her home for nine months. Inuit came aboard the vessel that morning to bid farewell to the missionary. Some inquired anxiously whether he would return the following year. Warmow told them, honestly but with some regret, that he could make no promise to return. And that was the last they would ever see of him or those of his faith.

A month later the *Lady Franklin* anchored off Aberdeen. A few days later Mathias Warmow was in London, where he made a preliminary report to the Secretaries to the Missions and the Committee of the Society for the Furtherance of the Gospel. From there he continued on to Herrnhut, Germany, the world headquarters of the church, and made his official report to the mission board.

The Moravians were businessmen as well as being men of God, and their efforts in Cumberland Sound were more in the nature of a feasibility study than a mission. Certainly Warmow was interested in the Inuit and in bringing a Christian message to them, but he also had a keen eye for how a permanent mission—were one ever to be established—would sustain itself. Their missions in Greenland and Labrador maintained themselves through the profits of their trading ventures. The big question for Warmow's mission board was: Would a mission to Baffin Island be able to pay its bills through trading?

After hearing of Warmow's time in Baffin Island, the board reluctantly concluded that it would not be possible to embark on a permanent mission to Cumberland Sound. They gave three reasons for their decision. The first was the small Inuit population; Warmow estimated the population of the sound to be 350, and decreasing. Unspoken but assumed was the fact that such a small population could not support enough trade activities to make a decent profit for the mission. Second, the activities of British and American whalers had created in the Inuit a dependence on the whaling industry. These activities had taken the Inuit away from their traditional camps and from their hunting and made them dependent on European foods and clothing totally unsuited to their circumstances. This in turn contributed to the population decline. The final reason was the difficulty the board thought it would encounter in supplying a mission and maintaining regular communication, especially if British whalers should cease to visit the sound.

Warmow had been touched by the desire of the Inuit to have a missionary in their midst. In his journal he wrote that, if a mission should be established there in the future, he would like "to live, and labour, and die among them." But it was not to be. On November 7 Warmow was ordained deacon; in January he married, and in

May he and his bride left Europe for his new mission at Lichtenau in southern Greenland. There, the next year, he wrote:

"I am often, in spirit, at Cumberland Inlet, and most heartily desire that a day of grace may soon come for the Esquimaux at that place."

The First
Inuktitut Language
Conference

I n the 1970s, under the auspices of Inuit Tapiriksat (now
Tapiriit) of Canada, the Inuit Language Commission
embarked on a major study of Canadian Inuit writing sys-
tems. This resulted in a standardization of the way Syllabics are
used and the adoption of a parallel alphabetic system.

What is less well known is that over one hundred years earlier, a meeting had been held in London, England, with the same
purpose—to standardize the writing of Inuktitut in Canada.
Although no Inuit were in attendance—in fact, there were only
two participants—this was the first Inuktitut language conference
ever held. This is the story of that important meeting.

The Syllabic writing system was created by James Evans for use among the Cree. The credit for adapting it to use in the writing of Inuktitut is usually given to Reverend Edmund James Peck, who arrived in Hudson Bay in the sub-Arctic in 1876. But the work of adaptation had in fact been done twenty years earlier by two missionaries of the Church Missionary Society: Reverend John Horden, working at Moose Factory, and Edwin Arthur Watkins, at Fort George and Little Whale River.

At the time Moose Factory, as well as being the trading centre of James Bay, was an intellectual hotbed, largely as a result of Horden's presence and his sincere interest in the Indian and Inuit people who traded there. Moreover, he had a printing press on which he published religious items for the instruction of the native people. He was a strong supporter of the Syllabic system as the means of bringing the Gospel to his parishioners.

In the winter of 1855–56 Horden printed a small book in Inuktitut for Watkins to use among the Inuit at Fort George. This book was written in Syllabics—the only Inuktitut Syllabic publication to come from Horden's press. It was, in fact, Inuktitut words written in Cree Syllabic script, complete with Cree finals.

In letters to the mission headquarters back in London, Watkins expressed some difficulty in bending the Cree system to fit the needs of Inuktitut. Horden, too, had written that the Inuit language placed a "very great strain on the system," and another missionary, T. H. Fleming, noted that "there are difficulties connected with it." In 1856 Horden and Watkins began to formally revise Syllabics to better suit Inuktitut, but their work was cut short when the missionary society transferred Watkins to Red River the following year.

In 1864 Henry Venn, the dynamic secretary of the Church Missionary Society, took the bull by the horns and decided that

In Those Days

Syllabics should be formally adapted, once and for all, to the Inuktitut language. He proposed a conference of Horden, Watkins, and a third missionary, Joseph Phelps Gardiner, who had worked among Indians and Inuit at Churchill. The conference would be held in London, and its purpose was "to promote an important object, the fixing of the Esquimaux language." But the ship on which Horden was to have left for England sank in James Bay, and the conference had to be postponed for one year. Unfortunately this meant that Gardiner could not be present. Nonetheless, in November of 1865, Horden and Watkins met under Venn's direction. The minutes of that mini-conference have survived. They are as follows:

1. It appears to us very undesirable that any changes, except such as are absolutely necessary, should be made in the Syllabarium as now used; though we quite agree that the system is not so scientifically accurate as could be wished....

2. In reducing the Esquimaux language into syllabic writing, we think that a change may be advantageously made in the final symbols. Instead of the arbitrary signs now in use for the Cree, we would propose the adoption of half-size characters of the same forms as those employed for the consonants in combination with the vowel a....

3. The additional consonants, b and d, found in the Esquimaux, may ... be represented ... by the characters for p and t respectively....

4. In the Esquimaux language there are some double consonants which will need to be represented. For these we

have adopted signs which combine as nearly as possible the two separate consonants.[1]

Horden and Watkins signed the minutes of this conference on November 24. The major revision adopted for Inuktitut was the standardization of the representation of syllable-final consonants, an adaptation that remains to this day.

Had Henry Venn not called this conference, it is doubtful that Inuktitut Syllabics would look like it does today, for in 1875 Horden wrote these words: "If the correction and improvement of the Syllabarium had been undertaken by me, as an individual, I would not say a word in its favour. I wished for no change, and only undertook the duty, in conjunction with Watkins, at the request, or rather command of Mr. Venn, who approved of the work when we had completed it."

---

[1] J. Horden and E. A. Watkins, "Minutes of a Conference by the Rev. J. Horden and E. A. Watkins on the subject of the syllabarium in use for the Cree and Esquimaux Languages," Benhall [England], 24 November 1865, cited from Church Missionary Society Archives, Microfilm Reel A-125.

Father Gasté's Remarkable Journey

When Samuel Hearne became the first white man to pass through the area of Nueltin Lake in the Kivalliq region in the late 1700s, there was as yet no Inuit presence there. It was not until the early 1800s that Inuit moved into that part of the interior. These Inuit, who came to be known as the Ahiarmiut, occupied an area tucked into the farthest southwest corner of what is today Nunavut.

Their culture was adapted to the interior. The mainstay of their existence was the barren-ground caribou, but fish from the numerous lakes also formed a good part of their diet. They lived at the edge of the northern forest. Pockets of spruce and tamarack grew along the Upper Kazan River, and the Ahiarmiut used this resource extensively. A biologist wrote in the 1940s, "The timber not only provided them with raw material for their sleighs [sleds], kayak frames, harpoons, drums, and various tools, but it also brought them into contact with various forest-inhabiting mammals and birds."

After establishing this isolated homeland, the Ahiarmiut traded into the Hudson's Bay Company's post at Churchill. But that pattern changed in 1868 as a result of a remarkable journey by a Roman Catholic priest.

Father Alphonse Gasté set out in April of that year from his base at Brochet on Reindeer Lake, southwest of Churchill and close to the present Manitoba-Saskatchewan border, accompanied by a number of Chipewyan hunters, on a proselytizing mission in which he hoped to visit the mysterious "Eskimos" of whom the Chipewyan had told him so much.

Finally, in early June, the travellers encountered their first Inuit. The priest recorded the meeting in these words:

> Early in the morning ... two young Montagnais [Chipewyan] had gone on a scouting trip. A little past noon, they returned with a band of Eskimo hunters and one or two old women of that nation.
>
> As soon as our Indians spied them from a distance, they wished them a hearty welcome according to the ceremonial in use among the Eskimos. They waved their blankets, imparting to them a circular motion. A few minutes later, our new visitors approached us with the traditional greeting of the North, that is to say, proferring their hands, they would repeat several times: "Taiman, taiman" which corresponds to our Good day.[1]

---

[1] Guy Mary-Rousselière, ed., "Father Gasté Meets the Inland Eskimos," *Eskimo*, Vol. 57 (December 1960) 6.

In Those Days

The two groups conversed by gestures, although it seems that one or two of the Chipewyan knew how to speak some Inuktitut.

This encounter was completely friendly. A century earlier, as Inuit had gradually displaced Chipewyan on the Hudson Bay coast, meetings were often hostile. Inuit had an unflattering name for the Chipewyan—*iqqiliit*, the ones with louse-eggs in their hair. Over time, suspicions and hostilities declined, and the two groups, at least in this small corner of Inuit territory, peacefully coexisted. Each summer the Chipewyans hunted north into the barren grounds, encountering Inuit on most of these forays, and there was generally caribou enough for all.

Father Gasté met with the Inuit on at least three occasions that summer. On the last one, about twenty hunters came to the Chipewyan camp. One man appeared to be the leader of this group. Gasté talked with him through a Chipewyan interpreter. "The Eskimo chief did not lack in intelligence," he wrote. "He even seemed to me to be practically the only one of his nation who had some notion of God and of our primitive traditions. I asked him how he had acquired them. He told me that it was during his journeys to Fort Churchill."

Gasté was frustrated at not being able to communicate more effectively with his newfound friends, and so he issued an invitation:

> As for me, seeing that my ministry was useless to these poor people, I wanted nonetheless to make some preparation for the future. So, I had the Eskimos assemble and, with an interpreter's help, invited them to frequent the Caribou Lake Fort [Brochet] in preference to Fort Churchill. I assured them, on the word of my Montagnais, that they would find it advantageous, as it was of easier access to them in their

journeys. It was agreed that, this year, five grown up men would come and visit our fort, explore the difficulties of the road and, if the advantage was proven, they would soon come in large numbers.[2]

Finally, in November, Father Gasté's six-month journey was at an end. He returned to his mission with forty hunters, including the five Inuit from the Upper Kazan.

"The most important result of this trip," he wrote, "the one that I had in mind when I set out, is that I had been able to maintain our Indians in their good disposition, to push ahead their instruction and, finally, to have paved the way for the evangelization of the Eskimos."

Inuit trading into Brochet lasted until about 1920. By then, adventurous white traders had begun to operate deep into the Kivalliq interior, near the north end of Nueltin Lake. From then on, it was no longer necessary for the Ahiarmiut to make the long trip deep into Chipewyan territory to Reindeer Lake.

---

[2] Ibid., 12–13.

Simon Gibbons

First Inuit Minister

Simon Gibbons's early years are lost in mystery. Indeed, one legend claims that he was found on an ice floe off the Labrador coast. The historical record is unclear, but he was probably born on June 21, 1851, to an Inuit woman in Forteau, Labrador, on the shores of the Strait of Belle Isle. Her name has not survived, and neither did she—one report is that she died while giving birth to Simon, another that she died a few years later. Simon's father was a white man, a fisherman named Thomas Gibbons.

A few years later Thomas Gibbons too was dead, leaving Simon, aged six, an orphan. He and his siblings were turned over to the "Widows and Orphans Asylum," run by the Church of England in St. John's. The orphanage reported that Simon "evinced intellect of no ordinary degree," and so he was placed in a school operated by the church. In 1862 his name came off the rolls of the orphanage when he was taken into the care of Sophia Mountain, widow of a minister, Jacob George Mountain. A few years later Mrs. Mountain remarried, to the bishop of Newfoundland, and Simon became a member of their household.

After graduation from the church academy, Simon continued his studies to prepare for the ministry, acting as lay reader, teacher, and catechist in some of Newfoundland's outports.

In 1875 he moved to Quebec, where he taught in a church-run academy at Clarenceville. Three years later he would return to that town to marry Frances, the rector's daughter, but before that he moved on to King's College in Windsor, Nova Scotia, where he prepared for ordination. Here, if he hadn't experienced it before, he had a taste of racism, being bullied by some of the other students because he was "different." He was a short, stocky man with a round face, swarthy complexion, straight black hair, and a moustache. Brushing the taunts of others aside, Gibbons persevered and was ordained deacon in February 1877 and priest a month later.

Simon Gibbons served as minister in three Nova Scotia parishes, the first in Victoria County, Cape Breton, where he acted as a travelling missionary. His trips were legendary and often dangerous. A biographer wrote, "More than once he would stumble into a friend's house … exhausted and with bloodstained snowshoes."

He also travelled to England to solicit money for the building of churches in Nova Scotia. Here he used his Inuit appearance to advantage. A church official wrote of him, "He had qualifications not possessed by every collector; a musical voice, fluent and eloquent speech, an attractive personality, and above all his thoroughly Eskimo physique. These attracted large audiences wherever he went." Gibbons summed it up simply in these words: "My face was my fortune." He preached in Westminster Abbey and had an audience with Queen Victoria.

He built and furnished two churches and a mission house with the money he raised on his first trip to England, as well as providing the bishop $4,500 to permanently endow the mission. The first church he completed was St. Andrew's-by-the-Sea at Neil's Harbour.

Exhausted after over seven years in Cape Breton, he transferred to Lockeport, Nova Scotia, where he ministered for three years to three congregations. But his health had deteriorated, and in 1885 he took a six-week vacation in the West Indies to recuperate. A few years later he returned to Britain for more fundraising. This trip too was successful, and he returned with funds and furnishings for his new church at Jordan Falls.

His last parish was Parrsboro, where he built three new churches. He worked along with the carpenters in their construction and served the workers a tot of rum each morning to encourage them.

Gibbons travelled and lectured extensively. He was a gifted and amusing speaker. One listener wrote, "Mr. Gibbons, who is one of the most humorous speakers that I have ever heard, convulsed the people with laughter and everyone went home in the best of humour." Gibbons apparently felt that an entertained listener gives more generously. He once remarked that "the Lord loves a hilarious giver."

His health continued to deteriorate, and he knew that his end was near. Shortly before his death, he said to a friend, "I shall not live much longer.... We Eskimos do not live to a great age. I am now forty-six, which is extremely old for an Eskimo. I do not believe that my changed habits and living conditions will prolong my life expectancy. I shall not live more than a few months longer at most." On the night of his death, December 14, 1896, he preached a sermon on the text "We needs must die." Then he went home and died. He and his wife had no children. He is buried in Parrsboro parish cemetery.

As with his birth, so legend also surrounds Gibbons in death. Bishop Leonard Hatfield wrote in 1987, "The ultimate legend about Simon Gibbons concerns a bird that often sits on the cross on top of the spire of St. George's Church at Parrsboro. It looks like a sea gull but is said to be the 'shade' of Simon Gibbons. It will not sit on any other church in town and it always faces north, back towards his home and his Eskimo people."

Joseph Lofthouse's Wedding Dilemma

J oseph Lofthouse had a problem. It was 1885. He was a missionary on the western coast of Hudson Bay and the only clergyman within five hundred miles. And he wanted to get married. More to the point, he needed to get married, for his fiancée had arrived on the annual ship intending to marry him immediately. Yet who would perform the ceremony?

Lofthouse had arrived in Hudson Bay as a single missionary in 1882. In a letter back to his mission board, he had lamented the fact that he travelled extensively, bringing the gospel to the Indians of the district, but that he had no wife with whom to share his life. The mission board took this as a suggestion that they should find a woman willing to travel to the wilds of Canada and share a life with Lofthouse. They found such a woman, a Miss Betsy Falding.

She was expected to arrive in 1884, so Lofthouse made the long trek from his mission at York Factory to Churchill to meet his fiancée, only to discover that she had been denied passage on the ship that year because there was no accommodation deemed suitable for a lady. Lofthouse returned home for another lonely winter. The following year the lady finally arrived aboard a Hudson's Bay Company ship, and Lofthouse was there to meet her.

He met his bride-to-be, whom he had never seen before, on the 28th of August, intending to marry her at once. He had expected that the Reverend G. S. Winters would be returning on the same ship and would perform the ceremony. But Winters's wife was ill in England, and his furlough had been extended for another year. That left Joseph Lofthouse as the only clergyman around.

In the past, in Hudson's Bay Company territory, marriages had sometimes been performed in the absence of a clergyman, by the factors in charge of trading posts. These marriages were done in the form of legal contracts, with declarations of consent, and in the presence of witnesses. But Lofthouse was not certain that it would be considered a legal marriage if there were a clergyman present but who had not performed the ceremony. The problem was that the only clergyman present was him.

He even considered the possibility of conducting his own marriage ceremony. As ridiculous as that may seem, a clergyman in the Mackenzie Delta once did just that, filling the roles of clergyman and groom in a ceremony in which he married a native woman. But Lofthouse ruled this out for his own case.

And then a solution presented itself. The Canadian government steamer *Alert* arrived with a scientific crew aboard. A meeting was held, and it was decided that Lieutenant Gordon, the commander of the Hudson Bay Expedition, was qualified to perform the ceremony. He had been commissioned a justice of the peace, and this gave him the necessary authority. Everyone attached to the ship and the trading post was present at the event on September 4. A marriage contract was written out and the service performed according to the practice of the Anglican Church. A wedding feast was held aboard the ship.

A few hours after the ceremony, Mr. and Mrs. Lofthouse left for York Factory aboard the HBC vessel *Cam Owen*. Bad weather resulted in this usually short trip taking fourteen days.

Joseph Lofthouse and his wife served many years together on the west coast of Hudson Bay. He went on to become Archdeacon of Moosonee, and in 1902 was ordained as the first Bishop of Keewatin. He died in 1933.

Taboos about Animals

Taboos about Sea Mammal Hunting

For most Inuit, the hunting of sea mammals was the very essence of Inuit livelihood. All the sea mammals had been created from the fingers of the sea spirit, and she demanded obedience to the taboos that had developed around these animals. The seal was the most important of these animals. It provided meat for food, skin for clothing, and fat to fuel the *qulliq*. For a people whose lives were dependent on this bounty of the sea, it was especially important to observe the many taboos associated with seal hunting and accord the animal the respect it deserved after a successful hunt.

Here are some of the taboos surrounding seals that had to be followed among the Iglulingmiut and the Aivilingmiut in pre-Christian times.

In Those Days

When a seal was brought into the house while the people were living in snow huts during the winter, no woman in the house could sew or do any other work until the seal had been cut up.

Before a newly caught seal had been cut up, no one could wipe rime from a windowpane, and no one could shake skins from the sleeping platform over the floor or straighten or rearrange the willow twigs that were under those skins. Care must also be taken not to spill any oil from the lamp, and no work could be done with stone, wood, or iron. Women could not comb their hair, wash their faces, or dry any footwear.

When seals were caught, one could not move camp the next day, but only two days after the catch. This was because the seals would be offended if the hunters did not show their gratitude by remaining in the same place.

When a seal was brought into a snow house, a lump of snow was dipped into the water bucket and then allowed to drip into the seal's mouth. It was said that the soul of the seal was drinking the water. But in summer the seal did not require water.

Persons hunting seal from a snow hut on the sea ice could not work with soapstone.

If a seal was brought into a house where a widow who had been widowed for not more than a year was present, then she must pull up her hood and not express her pleasure at the capture.

Young girls present in a house where a seal was being cut up had to take off their kamiks and remain barefoot while the work was in progress.

Men could cut up a seal at the ice edge if they intended to eat some of it there, but if a seal were brought home, it was the women who must cut it up.

When the seal was cut up and lay in pieces on the floor, a lump of fresh snow was laid on the spot where the head was and trodden down there by the men. The sea spirit did not like it if women trod on the spot where the head had lain.

The soul of a seal resides in the *naulaq*—the harpoon head—for one night after the seal has been killed. Therefore the harpoon head, with line and shaft, had to be taken into the house and placed beside the lamp when the hunter came home after a successful hunt. This was so that the soul of the seal might be warm throughout that first night while it remained in the harpoon that killed it.

Women must never make sinew from a ringed seal, a *natsiq*. Anyone who tried to sew with sinews made from a ringed seal would die because the sinews of the ringed seal are so short that the seal is ashamed of them, and its soul would kill anyone who tried to use them.

When a man who had lost his wife went out hunting and caught a seal for the first time, he had to observe a special taboo. He should cut up the carcass after three days, and he had to take the meat, but must leave the bones whole and also leave the entrails, skin, and blubber. He had to wrap the skin and blubber around the skeleton and place it on the ice as a sacrifice to the soul of his deceased wife. He must follow the same practice with the next two seals he took, except that he could do it immediately, without waiting three days. No stranger must eat from these first three seals, only the widower himself. Only once a fourth seal was caught was the death taboo removed.

When a bearded seal—*ugjuk*—was caught, a special sacrifice was required. Takannaaluk Arnaaluk (the Mother of the Sea Beasts) was particularly fond of bearded seals, and the animals knew it. So when they had been killed by humans, they went to her to complain. Therefore special precautions had to be taken when a bearded seal was taken.

As soon as the news went out that a bearded seal had been taken, the sleeping skins had to be made ready without delay, as they must then not be arranged for the next three days. During those three days, it was also forbidden to move camp.

In addition, no scraping of hair from skins could take place for three days after the capture of a bearded seal.

If a ringed seal or bearded seal was captured, all the women of the village must touch the meat of it with their index fingers.

Some places had special taboos. If a seal were caught in Tasiujaq, the great lake at Pingirqalik near Iglulik, the hunter must not work on hunting implements, neither making nor repairing them. He had also to cook his food in a special pot for a year after the capture. These were the same taboos that had to be observed by a man who had lost his brother. The severity of these taboos was because a seal taken there would be a freshwater seal—*qasigiaq*—and was thought not to be in its proper element, which should be salt water. The seal may have regarded this lake as a sanctuary. It was said that there was once a man who caught a seal there and failed to observe the taboo; although he had been perfectly healthy, he fell down dead soon after.

Hunting of sea mammals was dangerous, especially in open water from a kayak. But if the bird known as *saarvaq*, a small snipe, was placed in the bow of a kayak, the kayak-man would not upset in a heavy sea.

The first time a man paddled out in a newly covered kayak, his wife should put a cup of water on the place from where he embarked. This would give him good hunting, because the creatures of the sea were thought to be always thirsty.

Boys who had not yet caught bearded seals or walrus must not play at making string figures. Such a figure is called *ajaraq* in Inuktitut. In English it is often called a cat's cradle. Making them is a popular pastime in many cultures. But if boys who had not yet caught their first large sea mammal made these figures, they were liable to get their fingers tangled in the harpoon lines and be dragged into the sea. This taboo was reinforced by stories designed to convince boys not to while away their idle hours in making such figures.

Polar Bear Hunting Taboos

The polar bear was unique in the inventory of game that Inuit hunted. It bore its young in dens on land, but spent long periods of time hunting and travelling over sea ice and was comfortable even in the water. The taboos governing the bear hunt were, therefore, complex.

In Iglulik and Aivilik (the area of Repulse Bay, now called Naujaat), no work could be done by men or women for three days after a bear, a whale, or a bearded seal had been killed. This included a prohibition on cutting turf to use for fuel, because it came from the land. There were exceptions, though. For example, women were allowed to mend clothing, although making new articles of clothing was prohibited.

If a man returned with an animal that he had taken at the floe edge, he had to take off his outer clothing before entering his house.

Some special taboos had to be observed after successful bear hunts.

In Those Days

If a male bear was taken, its penis, bladder, spleen, and part of its tongue were hung up inside the house with the man's implements. After three days, the bear hunter had to take all these and throw them onto the floor of the house's entrance passage. The children had to then try to be the first to seize the implements and return them to their owner.

If the bear was a female, a sewing needle, thread, and an *ulu*—the woman's knife—were hung up with the bladder, the gall-bladder, and the spleen, also for three days. The number of days was significant because Inuit believed that the bear's soul only remained there for three days.

On returning to his house after killing a bear, a man had to take off all of his outer clothing, including his boots and mittens, before entering the house. He also had to refrain from eating meat or fat from the bear for a month.

If the bear's fat was used in the lamps for cooking or lighting, then the occupants of that house could not crack marrow bones or eat the delicious marrow.

Among many groups of Inuit were people who had resorted to cannibalism to preserve their own lives. An important taboo applied to the behaviour of these people. They were never to eat bear meat because it was said to taste so much like human flesh.

Caribou Taboos

To many Inuit, the caribou was the most important of all the animals they hunted. It provided food, material for clothing, and sinew thread for sewing. Special rules that governed its hunting were therefore very important and very complicated.

For Inuit in the Iglulik and Repulse Bay areas, caribou hunting began in early July, when seal hunting on the ice had effectively ended. Camps would be relocated inland and Inuit would often remain there throughout the fall, until hunting on the sea ice could resume.

Very strong rules governed the seasonal and geographic line between hunting for caribou and hunting for sea mammals. Women were most important in maintaining these taboos; their proper behaviour was paramount in seeing that no infractions of acceptable behaviour took place.

No new garments could be made while a hunting party and their families were living in tents—only once they had moved into snow houses could sewing of caribou skins take place. If it was an absolute necessity that a man should have a new hunting coat before a proper snow house could be made, then a temporary snow shelter could be constructed, just large enough for the woman to do her sewing.

Orulo, wife of the shaman Aua, said, "When the caribou have shed their old coats and the new ones have come, material of sealskin and used for footwear must no longer be used. If there are men who must absolutely have new soles to their boots, then the sole leather must be laid out on the floor to be trodden on, so that it is no longer new, but soiled, and old kamiks may then be soled, but the work must be done out of doors, not in the tent."

A family that was inland hunting caribou could not return to the coast and go onto the sea ice to begin hunting sea mammals until all necessary caribou skin items had been made; this included all outer and inner clothing and sleeping skins.

At Iglulik, it was permitted for some men to hunt walrus even

In Those Days

when the women had not finished making the winter clothes, but their snow huts had to be built on the land and never on the ice, and only three men from a village could participate in the hunt. They were, furthermore, not allowed to eat caribou head or marrow, but could eat the meat of the animal as long as it was frozen—never boiled. And even then, they could only eat it while wearing mittens!

The observance of taboos was believed to be especially necessary at Iglulik because it was from there that people supposed that the sea spirit, Takannaaluk Arnaaluk, had resided before descending to the depths of the ocean. There, it was forbidden to eat the flesh of walrus, whale, or seal on the same day as caribou meat, nor was caribou meat allowed in the house at the same time as the meat of those sea mammals.

No walrus meat could be brought indoors as long as caribou-skin garments were being made. And walrus hide, or anything made from it, could not be taken inland when hunting caribou. Harpoon lines of bearded seal, though, could be used, as long as they had not previously been used for walrus hunting.

Autumn skins of caribou killed inland, and their meat, could not be brought into a snow hut on the sea ice through the normal passage entrance; instead, a hole must be cut in the back of the house above the sleeping place.

All of the taboos designed to separate the use of caribou products and the skins and meat of sea mammals came to an end when the seals had their young in the spring. Spring, with the return of the sun, brought not only light and warmth but also liberation from a long list of irrational taboos. The season must have been especially appreciated by the women of every hunting camp.

Taboos and Beliefs about Earth Eggs

There are many other beliefs associated with caribou, that most important of land animals. One belief concerns a type of egg that could occasionally be found on the land during spring.

These eggs were called *silaqsait* (*silaqsaq* in the singular), which is often rendered into English as "earth eggs." (The spelling varies. Some accounts give the words as *silaaqsaq* and *silaaqsait*.)

Francois Quassa, an Igloolik elder, told a visiting anthropologist in the early 1990s that these eggs were solitary, never found in nests, and were often bluish in colour, and that people "were warned to be careful of the *silaqsait*," because they contained the children of *sila*, the powerful spirit that governed the weather. In most accounts, the animal that could hatch from an earth egg would be an albino caribou, but it was also possible for the egg to hatch into a bearded seal, a polar bear, or another animal. If one were to break such an egg or kill a hatchling, said Noah Piugaattuk, another elder from Igloolik, bad weather would ensue.

Quassa also remembered that someone had recently crushed such an egg accidentally, and that as a result the weather was bad for a whole year. Others attributed thick fog and heavy rain to the inadvertent breaking of a *silaqsaq*.

In Pond Inlet in 1957, an Inuk told a Catholic priest about the white caribou that was believed to hatch from the earth eggs: "We call them 'ground eggs' because they are produced in the ground. The sun, during the spring, warms them up and makes them hatch. Not any bigger than a goose's egg, their shell breaks only at the end of the season. A small, very small caribou comes out, but he grows very fast. These caribous remain white summer and winter."

In Those Days

The late Felix Kuppaq of Repulse Bay, who passed away in 2005, gave a detailed account of finding an earth egg to the anthropologists Frédéric Laugrand and Jarich Oosten: "I, too, have come across an earth egg on the side of a *niaquptaq*, a clump of moss. It was not too big; it was smaller than a seagull's egg and rounder, but larger than the egg of a *pitsiulaaq*, a black guillemot. It was on its side and protruding out of the ground. I took it and tried to make sure I didn't disturb the earth around it. Part of it was brown and dark. That's the pattern that it had. It was rounder than a bird's egg. I took it home."

His mother asked him where the egg had come from and told him it was an earth egg and that it might turn into a wolverine or even a muskox, because of its dark colour. His father told him that "if it was going to become a hare or a polar bear, it would have been white." His parents told Felix to return it to where he had found it.

"So I put it back where I found it and went home again," he continued. "After I got home, it started raining for five days. Maybe if I had actually broken it, the rain would have been a lot worse."

In the early 1920s, the shaman Aua told Knud Rasmussen in detail about the giant caribou that could hatch from a *silaqsaq* (Rasmussen spelled it *silaasaat* in the plural):

> There are in the earth large white eggs ... as big as the bladder of a walrus. They turn to *silaat* or *silaaraaluit*. These *silaaraaluit* are, when fully developed, shaped almost like caribou, but with large snouts, hair like that of a lemming, and legs as tall as tent poles. They look as if they were as big as an *umiaq*, but they are not dangerous—they have the nature of the caribou. Their foot-marks are so large that

84

two hands with outstretched fingers will not cover one. If it is killed, and one wishes to cut it up, it will take several days, so great are these animals.... When one of these giant beasts is seen among caribou, it appears like a white mountain of snow. When it takes to flight and treads the ground, rain falls, pouring, drenching rain, and a thick mist covers the earth.[1]

Aua told Rasmussen that he had seen such an animal at close quarters, and seen it take flight along with terrified caribou.

Aua knew that these stories stretched people's belief. He explained, "To speak of them or describe them is like lying, no one believes it, but it is nevertheless true. They are called *silaq* ... and this means something of *sila*, of the earth, of the universe, of the air, of the weather. It is said that they are the children of the earth. Anyone killing such a *silaq* must observe the same taboo as a man who has lost his brother."

The belief in the existence of earth eggs continues to this day.

---

[1] Knud Rasmussen, *Intellectual Culture of the Iglulik Eskimos. Report of the Fifth Thule Expedition 1921–24.* Vol VII, No. 1 (Copehagen: Gyldendalske Boghandel, 1929), 202.

Edmund Peck

Missionary to the Inuit

In 1875 Bishop John Horden wrote from Moose Factory to the Church Missionary Society (CMS) in England asking them to send a missionary to Canada to work with the Inuit of Hudson Bay. Edmund James Peck, an unordained seaman, accepted the challenge, underwent brief training, and departed for Hudson Bay in June 1876.

Peck had been born in Rusholme, England, on April 15, 1850, but was raised from the age of seven in Ireland, where he developed an antipathy towards Catholicism. By thirteen he was an orphan, and he joined the British Navy soon after, serving for eight years.

Horden sent him to Little Whale River, where he ministered to both Cree and Inuit. Peck set himself an arduous program for learning the languages of both, believing that "the first work of every missionary is to acquire the language of the people as well as gain their confidence." He concentrated, however, on Inukti-tut and claimed to have collected between eighty and one hundred words per day. Modern-day language students might find it an outrageous claim, but it was possible in an isolated post, with none of the distractions that plague today's learners.

Part of Peck's mandate from the CMS was to produce written religious material, and he approached this task eagerly, using the Syllabic system of writing created by James Evans in 1840 for the Cree and modified for Inuktitut by CMS missionaries Horden and E. A. Watkins. Peck was the first missionary in Hudson and James bays to work almost exclusively with Inuit. He promoted the use of Syllabics, transcribed Moravian church materials from the Labrador coast into the new script, and taught reading and writing skills to the Inuit. His first Inuktitut publication, *Portions of the Holy Scripture, for the use of the Esquimaux on the northern and eastern shores of Hudson's Bay*, was printed in the Syllabic orthography by the Society for the Promotion of Christian Knowledge (SPCK) in 1878.

Peck took furlough in England in 1884 after eight uninterrupted years in the field. He returned with a bride the following year, and the next year relocated his mission two hundred miles south to Fort George. The Pecks had three children there, but Mrs. Peck was often sick and depressed, and in 1892 the family returned to England. Two years later, SPCK published Peck's second major work in Inuktitut, *Portions of the Book of Common Prayer, together with hymns, addresses, etc., for the use of the Eskimo of Hudson's Bay*.

In England Peck immediately began making plans to establish a mission in Baffin Island. His wife's health was sufficiently poor, he reasoned, that she would never be able to accompany him again to the Arctic, and therefore he should leave already-established missions to other married men and go instead to isolated and undeveloped areas where he felt no woman should go.

So in 1894, with the assistance of Crawford Noble, the Scottish owner of whaling stations in Cumberland Sound, Peck established a mission at Blacklead Island. The whalers provided Peck and his assistant, Joseph Parker, spartan living quarters in a two-room shack, each room ten feet square. The Inuit to whom Peck would minister lived nearby in a camp of skin tents and ramshackle wooden huts. Their population numbered 171.

Peck found little difference between the dialect that he had mastered in Hudson Bay and that of Cumberland Sound, and he began immediately to preach the gospel and teach the children. He maintained a disciplined routine of teaching, studying, and preaching. He faced opposition to his ministry from Inuit shamans, whom he regarded as sly tricksters and against whom he spoke out openly and strongly. The missionary persevered, and eventually all the Inuit of Cumberland Sound were converted to at least a nominal acceptance of Christianity.

Edmund Peck spent four periods of two years each at Blacklead Island. It was a spartan and disciplined life. Here was his schedule for most days:

Rise 6:45 a.m., light fires, prepare breakfast; breakfast 8 a.m.; prayers 8:30 a.m.; study of Eskimo language … from 9 a.m. to 10 a.m.; visiting and preparing Eskimo addresses from 10 a.m. to noon. Then came the preparation of dinner. Dinner 1 p.m.; private reading and study from 2 p.m. to 3 p.m.; school for children from 3 p.m. to 4:15 p.m.; visiting and exercise from 4:15 to 5:30 p.m.; after tea, prepare for evening meeting, which is at 7:30 p.m.; after the meeting, study of the language with Eskimos; prayer at 10 p.m.; then private reading and devotion till 10:45 p.m. This ended the day and bed had been earned.[1]

The schedule for Sunday was different, calling for religious services in his small church. Other than that, this rigorous schedule was broken only by the occasional sled trip to Kekerten, a whaling station across the sound from Blacklead Island.

On each of his one-year furloughs to England, Peck continued working to oversee the publication of church literature in Syllabics, lecture publicly about the importance of his mission to the Inuit, and lobby the mission society for the mission's continuance. Other missionaries, whose terms generally overlapped Peck's, maintained the mission during his absences. Their names are well known in the history of Northern missions: Charles Sampson, Julian Bilby, and E. W. T. Greenshield.

Peck left Blacklead Island permanently in 1905. The following year, with the departure of Greenshield, the mission was left with no resident non-native minister. But Peck and his colleagues had trained a number of Inuit catechists, the most well known being Luke Killaapik and Peter Tulugarjuaq. When Greenshield returned on a summer voyage in 1909, on which he was shipwrecked and forced to spend the winter, he discovered that these native catechists had faithfully continued the work of the mission.

Peck moved his family to Ottawa, where he became Superintendent of Arctic Missions for the Diocese of Moosonee. Occasionally he travelled north on supply vessels in the summer, usually

---

[1] Arthur Lewis, *The Life and Work of the Rev. E. J. Peck among the Eskimos* (London: Hodder & Stoughton, 1904), 214–15.

to Hudson Bay. His eyesight failed and, almost blind, he retired in 1919. He died in Ottawa in 1924.

Although Peck is often credited with adapting Evans's Cree Syllabics to Inuktitut, that innovation had already been made by Horden and Watkins. Peck's great accomplishment was proselytizing among the Inuit, promoting the use of the Syllabic orthography, and translating and publishing scripture material in Inuktitut. He promoted literacy in Syllabics. Following his lead, all Anglicans who followed him in the eastern Arctic used the Syllabic orthography, as did Roman Catholic missionaries. The Syllabic orthography is still used today in Arctic Quebec and all but a few western communities of Nunavut. Occasionally debate occurs about its continued efficacy in promoting Inuktitut literacy in an increasingly bilingual population, but such debates are usually short-lived—the Syllabics that Peck promoted are viewed by now as being the traditional Inuit way of writing in the eastern Canadian Arctic.

Peck's contributions to the study of the Inuktitut language are contained in two works: his *Eskimo Grammar*, published by the Geographic Board of Canada in 1919 and subsequently reprinted four times, and his *Eskimo-English Dictionary*, published posthumously in 1925.

Inuit remember Peck, whose Inuktitut name, Uqammak, means "the one who speaks well," as a dogmatic and tenacious man, at once stubborn yet caring, stern yet friendly. Non-native history remembers him as "The Apostle to the North." In 1877, one year after Peck's arrival in Canada, Bishop John Horden wrote to the Church Missionary Society about Peck, "I thank the Committee for *a* man; I thank them doubly for *the* man; a better selection could not have been made."

The Blacklead Island Mission

Preaching in a Sealskin Church

When Reverend Edmund James Peck—Uqammak to the Inuit—
and his assistant, Joseph Parker, arrived on Blacklead Island in
Cumberland Sound off the east coast of Baffin Island in the summer of 1894, they took up their quarters in a building that had been
provided to them by the Scottish whaling company operating there.
The building was nothing more than a two-room shack, really, only
two hundred square feet in size. They had not only to live in it, but
also to cram their year's supply of perishable goods into it. Those
supplies included: 1 ton of flour, 800 pounds of sugar, 180 pounds
of tea, 800 pounds of preserved meats, dried and preserved vegetables, 600 pounds of oatmeal, 1 ton of biscuits, 100 pounds of jam,
1 barrel of paraffin oil, methylated spirits, articles of trade including
knives, pipes, tobacco, and scissors, and 200 pounds of soap.

In Those Days

Although there were a number of Scottish whalers on the island, Peck and Parker had come to minister to the Inuit. Some time after their arrival, Peck took a census and found that there were 171 people living on the small island, in some forty tents.

Immediately the two missionaries established a routine, which they generally followed rigidly unless they were travelling. Much of it centred around the learning of Inuktitut. Peck already spoke the language from his almost two decades of missionary work on the Quebec coast, but Parker was new to the North and to the language. Peck had not only to learn the nuances of the Blacklead Island dialect that differentiated it from that of Quebec, but also to instruct Parker in the basics of the language.

The cramped quarters the two men shared were too small to accommodate many visitors, and they badly needed a separate place of worship. The solution to their problem was ingenious, and it was provided by the Blacklead Inuit themselves. They constructed a large tent of sealskin. Indeed, it was so large that Peck referred to it as a sealskin "tabernacle."

Peck wrote: "Our church—if such it can be called—is twenty feet long and about ten feet wide. It is made principally of seal skins sewn together, which skins are stretched on a frame and seats are placed inside on which the people sit in rows." In a letter to his mission society, he wrote, "When I mention the encouraging fact that the whole structure was erected, and to a great measure planned, by the Eskimos themselves, friends will readily see that we have every reason to thank God, and toil on for his people's salvation without doubt or despondence."

Peck held his first service in the sealskin church on Sunday, October 7. For him, it was "a very happy but wearing day." In his journal, he wrote that "we visited the people from tent to tent, and invited them to come to our opening meeting. Many came, and they joined heartily in the few hymns they knew."

The sealskin church served its purpose for a few months until shortly after the new year. Then a period of poor hunting and extreme hunger affected all the inhabitants of Blacklead, both men and dogs. At 3 a.m. on January 23, Peck and Parker were awakened by the sound of a pack of starving dogs on top of the church; they were tearing it to pieces. Peck estimated there were over one hundred of the ravenous animals. Many had fallen through the roof into the church. They destroyed a good portion of it.

Parker wrote in his diary: "We were quickly on the scene of destruction, but too late to be able to save much of the materials which had formed the roof.... It was a sorry little edifice—still, our best. Next day we set to and repaired it somehow with all kinds of odds and ends, so that it was in use again the following day. It has undergone repairs and improvements this summer, but still remains a despicable little object, though I am glad to say the people think it grand."

On one of his fundraising visits to Scotland, he told the story of the sealskin church to a Sunday school class. A young girl remarked, "Now that we have heard of a kirk being eaten by dogs, it is not hard to believe that a whale could have swallowed Jonah."

Tragedy at Blacklead Island

When Edmund Peck had approached the Church Missionary Society with his plan to open a mission at the isolated whaling station at Blacklead Island, the society approved his plan, but with one condition. Peck could not go out alone—he must find a partner to share the work with him. Joseph Caldecott Parker, a twenty-two-year-old layman, volunteered for the task.

Parker had enrolled at CMS's Preparatory Institute in February of 1891 but had withdrawn a year later because his father was seriously ill. In 1893 he expressed his interest in accompanying Peck to Cumberland Sound and spent a few months preparing for the task at Church Missionary College. There he received some medical training, a distinct advantage in the isolated region for which he was bound.

In 1894 the two missionaries signed on as members of the eight-man crew of the *Alert*, a vessel of 129 tons, 90 feet in length. Peck joined as chaplain, Parker as doctor. Defying the superstitions of whaling tradition, the vessel left Peterhead on Friday, the 13th of July.

Joseph Parker made rapid progress in learning the Inuktitut language. He attended to the sick, and the Inuit rewarded him with the name Luuktakuluk—"the little doctor." In 1896 he began work, as so many missionaries do, on an Inuktitut-language dictionary. Unfortunately, a tragic accident prevented him from ever finishing it.

In August, shortly before the expected arrival of the annual supply vessel, Parker joined a group of men leaving Blacklead in a small boat to go fishing at a river about twenty miles away. The other men were a whaler known as Captain Clisby; Crawford Noble's agent, Alexander Hall; and four Inuit. That evening Peck sat alone in his mission house reading a section from Chapter 20 of Acts of the Apostles, a passage telling of St. Paul's farewell address to the elders of the Ephesian church. Suddenly he felt "almost overcome with most solemn feelings accompanied with a tender constraining sense of love to the Lord Jesus, and affection to Mr. Parker." Perhaps this was a harbinger of an unfolding tragedy—the Bible passage ends with Paul's final words as the faithful saw him off on a ship, "You will never see me again."

Three days later, on August 14, Peck was digging for clams on a tidal flat off Naujartalik Island, three miles from the station, when an Inuk arrived by kayak. He had found a boat adrift, with the body of Captain Clisby inside. Peck and his Inuit companions immediately rowed northward and found the boat. Clisby indeed lay dead inside. The boat was towed to Blacklead Island and a search party left to look for any trace of the other members of the fishing party. Nothing was found, and everyone, including Parker, was assumed to have drowned.

Peck had planned to return to England on furlough in 1896. Parker's death very nearly caused him to change his mind. But when the *Alert* arrived only a week after the tragedy, it brought another missionary, Charles Sampson. Peck learned that the new man also had some medical experience. Sampson quickly showed an ability to learn Inuktitut. In mid-September a small steamer, the *Hope*, unexpectedly arrived at the station. She had been chartered by the American explorer Robert Peary for a summer voyage to Greenland and was on her return leg. Peck took passage on her to Sydney, Nova Scotia, where he caught another ship to England.

While in Sydney, Peck wrote a letter to CMS, informing them of the tragedy:

And now with feelings of deep sorrow I must tell you the sad news of our dear brother Parker's death. He was drowned near Blacklead Island on the 11th of August. Mr. Hall (Mr. Noble's agent) had arranged to go to a river some twenty miles from the station to catch salmon, and as our brother had been working most assiduously at the study of language, etc., and as he needed a change and rest he thought it well … to join the party.

I cannot say exactly how the sad accident happened, but we suppose that a squall struck the boat after she passed out of sight on the northern side of the island. We think the boat must have then heeled over, and the boom of sail was thus caught in the sea to leeward, and while the boat was thus held down a sea rushed in and swamped her.

I feel that I have lost a real friend and brother in Mr. Parker. He was, in every sense of the word, a true helper, and one who, I may truly say, poured out his whole energies on the work which God had given him to do.[1]

The First Baptism

When Peck arrived at Blacklead Island in 1894, the Inuit population there was 171, a huge number of Inuit to find congregated at any one spot, but they were there because of the presence of a Scottish whaling station and the seasonal employment that brought. With that also came crowded conditions in tents and wooden shacks, exploitation at the hands of some unscrupulous whalers, and disease, including tuberculosis—or consumption, as it was known at the time.

---

[1] Letter, Edmund Peck to Mr. Stack, Church Missionary Society, Sydney, Nova Scotia, 28 September 1896. 1896-152. Church Missionary Society Archives, Microfilm Reel A-119.

Peck set to work to bring Christianity to the people. He translated portions of the scriptures and established a school and even a small medical facility, which he dignified with the term "hospital." And he looked forward to the day when he would baptize his first convert. But he took his time. He would not baptize for the sake of numbers. Those who would be baptized had to be sincere believers in the teachings Peck brought to them. The first baptism was not until seven years after his arrival.

In April of 1901, a young woman named Atungaujaq makes her first appearance in Peck's diary. She had taken the name Annie. On April 8 Atungaujaq was sick, and Peck visited her in her home. He thought that she seemed to be wasting away from consumption. He was impressed with the young lady. She had learned a great deal about the gospel, and she listened with rapt attention as the missionary exhorted her to "trust wholly in the Saviour."

Almost a month later, her condition having deteriorated, she told Peck that she wished to be baptized. Peck wrote, "I see no reason why the rite should be withheld from her. We claim this poor creature for Christ. I have been and am much helped in prayer concerning her."

That same day she had a violent attack of bleeding from the lungs. Peck succeeded in checking it, and later he baptized her privately. He noted that "she was pleased; but said that if spared she would like to be received publicly." There were other female candidates for baptism; he spoke with them about her and was satisfied to learn that one of the women visited her regularly and prayed with her.

He decided to publicly baptize Atungaujaq. She was too weak to be taken to the tiny church that Peck had constructed on the island, so the service was conducted outside, behind a windbreak of snow, at the entrance to her dwelling. On May 7 Peck's congregation gathered there with Annie Atungaujaq and "dedicated her again to God." He described her as "the first fruits of what we trust will be a mighty harvest of souls."

Spring came slowly to the windswept island. On June 12 the missionary wrote in his journal, "Four beautiful little flowers seen today." The following day, Annie Atungaujaq finally succumbed to her illness. Peck noted, "Annie A. fell asleep today." The missionary had visited her regularly until the end. "I was with her when she passed away," he wrote. "She was quite conscious, but a calm and peaceful look spread over her face as the Spirit returned to Him who gave it."

Peck wanted to provide a proper burial. The books he had provided the Inuit contained the Burial Service in Inuktitut, and his congregation followed as he read from it in the church. Then they went to the gravesite that her relatives had selected. "I do not mean that a grave was dug," he wrote. "This we cannot do. There is no soil here deep enough.... Our burial places must therefore be on the rocks." Peck's fellow missionary, Julian Bilby, had constructed a coffin, stones were placed on top of it, and Peck concluded the service with "a few solemn words to those assembled." He noted the difference between this Christian burial and "the awful way in which some of the dead have been buried—no covering but the snow and the carcase [sic] torn to pieces by the dogs as soon as they could reach it."

Peck and Bilby had not yet succeeded in bringing the whole population of Blacklead to Christianity, however. Three days later he noted in his journal, "An old woman died today, the heathen carrying on their incantations till the last. So the battle rages between the powers of light and darkness."

Julian Bilby and Annie Sikuliaq: A Missionary and His Lover

Julian William Bilby was born in England in 1871, the son of a schoolmaster. Little is known of his childhood. He worked as a cabinetmaker before joining the Church Missionary Society in 1895 and went out to Blacklead Island three years later.

Bilby was unusual for a missionary, constantly at odds with the mission office in London and openly critical of the mission's dependence on the Scottish whalers who ran a station at Blacklead. CMS could not afford to charter its own ships, and so the missionaries were reliant on the whalers for transportation. Others took this as a signal that the missionaries should be muted in their criticism of the whalers, many of whom had relationships with Inuit women despite their traditional marriages to women back home. But Bilby was outspokenly critical.

He first arrived at the mission in 1898, four years after Edmund Peck had established it. Peck was there, halfway through his second stint, when Bilby arrived. So was another missionary who would later court controversy, Charles Sampson.

The following summer, Peck left for England, leaving Bilby and Sampson alone at Blacklead. He returned to his post in 1900, and Sampson left that summer. Bilby remained for another year with Peck before taking furlough in England.

In 1902 Bilby returned to Blacklead while Peck again went to England for one year. Bilby remained at the mission, this time for three years.

Peck was unusual among CMS clergymen in advocating that missionaries should be free to marry native women. He was happily married to an English woman who had been with him in his

Quebec ministry but remained in England during his four stints at Blacklead. But he felt that adopting a liberal policy of allowing young missionaries to "marry local" was the only way that the church would be able to recruit and retain men at the society's far-flung posts throughout the world. Of course, what he had in mind were church-sanctioned marriages performed by ordained clergymen. He had not anticipated that a missionary might take an Inuit woman as a wife through local custom marriage.

Yet, apparently, that is exactly what Bilby did at some point before his departure for England in 1905. Three decades ago Qattuuq Evic, an elderly woman in Pangnirtung, recounted that Bilby, whom she remembered as being not as popular as Peck or Greenshield, "was the only one who married while in Cumberland Sound." The object of his affections was Annie Sikuliaq, the sister of Tulugarjuaq, a native catechist whom Peck had trained and who was one of the stalwart supporters of the new faith that was replacing traditional beliefs in the sound. Tulugarjuaq was an influential man. He had converted to Christianity and was appointed the first native teacher at Blacklead. The fact that Bilby lived with his sister can probably be taken to mean that Tulugarjuaq sanctioned the relationship.

But Bilby left Blacklead in the summer of 1905. Was this at the suggestion of Peck? Or of the officials at CMS headquarters? The written record is silent on the reasons. Perhaps it was simply time for a furlough.

The next summer it was the turn of Reverend E. W. T. Greenshield to go to England for a holiday at the end of his second term on Blacklead. He travelled on the Dutch-registered vessel *Jantina Agatha*, which Crawford Noble, the whaling station owner, had chartered that year. Its destination was Aberdeen.

FIGURE 1: "Mother of the sea animals," known to Inuit as Sedna, Nuliajuk, Taliilajuq, Uinigumasuittuq, or Takannaaluk Arnaaluk. This drawing was made by the shaman Anarqaaq for Knud Rasmussen on the Fifth Thule Expedition.

SOURCE: KNUD RASMUSSEN, *INTELLECTUAL CULTURE OF THE IGLULIK ESKIMOS, REPORT OF THE FIFTH THULE EXPEDITION 1921–24,* VOLUME VII, NO. 1. COPENHAGEN: GYLDENDALSKE BOGHANDEL, 1929.

FIGURE 2: Sedna is at the heart of Inuit mythology. Cast overboard by her father in a storm, her fingers amputated as she clung to the side of the boat, she sank to the bottom of the sea, where sea mammals become entangled in her hair. She controls their supply to the hunters who depend on them.
SOURCE: GERMAINE ARNAKTAUYOK, *SEDNA—THE STORM* AND *SEDNA—THE RULER* (DIPTYCH). 1994, ETCHING/AQUATINT, 14" × 16".

FIGURE 3: The Hvalsey Church in Greenland near Qaqortoq. A marriage took place there in 1408; it is the last dated reference to the Norse in Greenland.

SOURCE: ARKTISK INSTITUT, ID 17819.

FIGURE 4: Martin Frobisher commanded the 1578
expedition to Frobisher Bay, on which the first
Thanksgiving service in North America was held.
SOURCE: THE BODLEIAN LIBRARY, UNIVERSITY OF OXFORD,
L.P. 50.

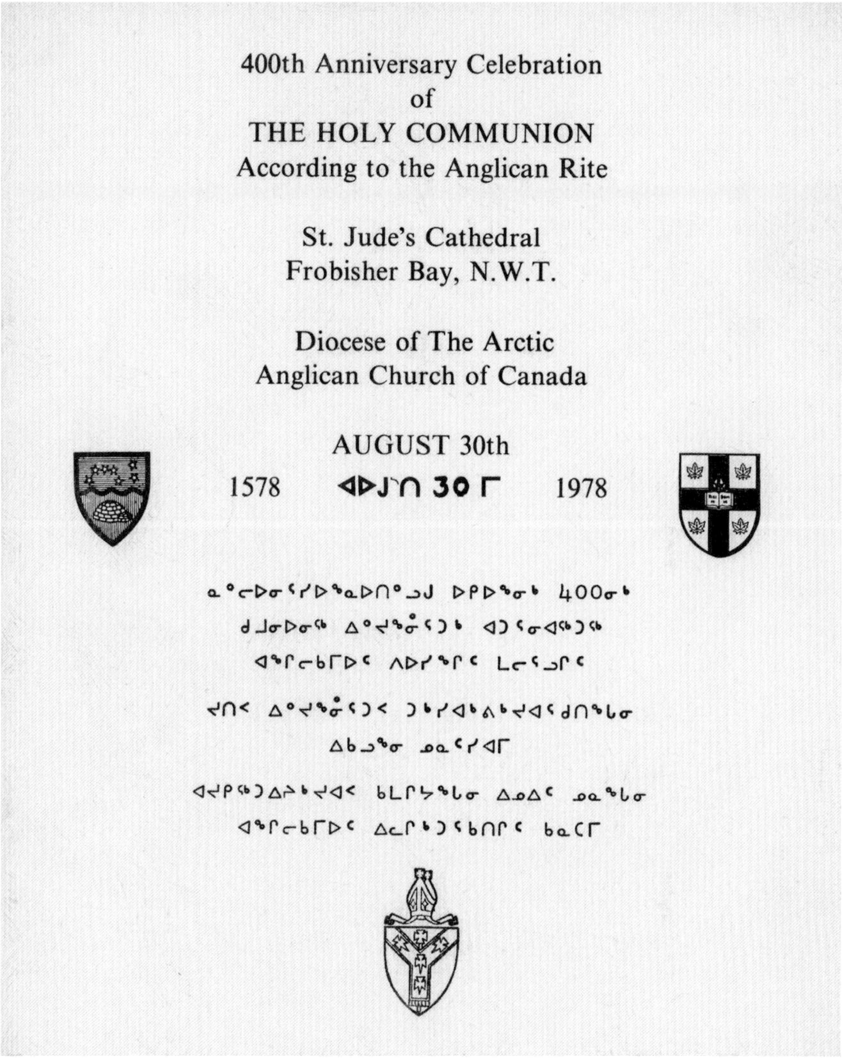

400th Anniversary Celebration
of
THE HOLY COMMUNION
According to the Anglican Rite

St. Jude's Cathedral
Frobisher Bay, N.W.T.

Diocese of The Arctic
Anglican Church of Canada

AUGUST 30th

 1578　　ᐊᐅᒡᑎ **30** ᒋ　　1978

ᖃᓄᑐᐁᓯᐲᐅᖁᐊᐳᏁᐅ ᒍᒍᐃᐃ ᐅᑦᐅᖁᐅ 400ᐅ•
ᒡᒍᒑᐳᖅ ᐊᐟᐅᖃᓐᑐ• ᐊᒐ ᐟᖃᐊᑫᒑ
ᐊᐲᕈᑲᒥᐳᐨ ᐱᐅᐧᐲᕈᐨ ᒪᕈᐟᒍᕈᐨ

ᐟᐢᐨ ᐊᐤᐟᐅᖃᐟᑐᐨ ᒍᐧᕈᐊᐧᐱᐧᐟᐊᐨᒡᑎᐧᒪᐪ
ᐃᑲᒍᐧᐅ ᐳᐊᐨᕈᐊᒥ

ᐊᐟᐸᐧᒍᐊᐣᐧᐧᐅᐨ ᑲᒪᕈᐧᐧᒪᐪ ᐅᐤᐃᐨ ᐳᐊᐧᒪᐪ
ᐊᐲᕈᑲᒥᐳᐨ ᐃᑲᕈᐧᒍᐧᐟᑲᐧᕈᐨ ᑲᐅᕈᒍ

FIGURE 5: In 1978 the Diocese of the Arctic celebrated the 400th anniversary of the first Holy Communion—and the first Thanksgiving—in North America.
SOURCE: KENN HARPER COLLECTION.

FIGURE 6: Otto Fabricius, whose Greenlandic name was Erisaalik. Although Fabricius lived in Greenland for only six years in the 1700s, he wrote extensively about Greenland and compiled an impressive grammar and dictionary of Kalaallisut.

SOURCE: ERIK HOLTVED. *OTTO FABRICIUS' ETHNOGRAPHICAL WORKS, MEDDELELSER ON GRØNLAND, VOLUME 140, NO. 2*, COPENHAGEN: C. A. REITZELS FORLAG, 1962. FRONTISPIECE. (KENN HARPER COLLECTION.)

Forsøg

til

en, forbedret

Grønlandsk Grammatica

ved

Otho Fabricius,

Sognepræst ved Vor Frelseres Kirke paa Christianshavn.

Kiøbenhavn, 1791.
Trykt udi det Kongelige Waysenhuses Bogtrykkerie,
af Carl Friderich Schubart.

FIGURE 7: Otto Fabricius published a grammar of Greenlandic in 1791. Most copies were destroyed in a warehouse fire in Copenhagen. As a result, it is very rare.
SOURCE: KENN HARPER COLLECTION.

FIGURE 8: Samuel Kleinschmidt standardized the Greenlandic orthography in the 1850s, bringing literacy to the population. This engraving is from a photograph taken in 1885, a year before his death.
SOURCE: ARKTISK INSTITUT, ID 15188.

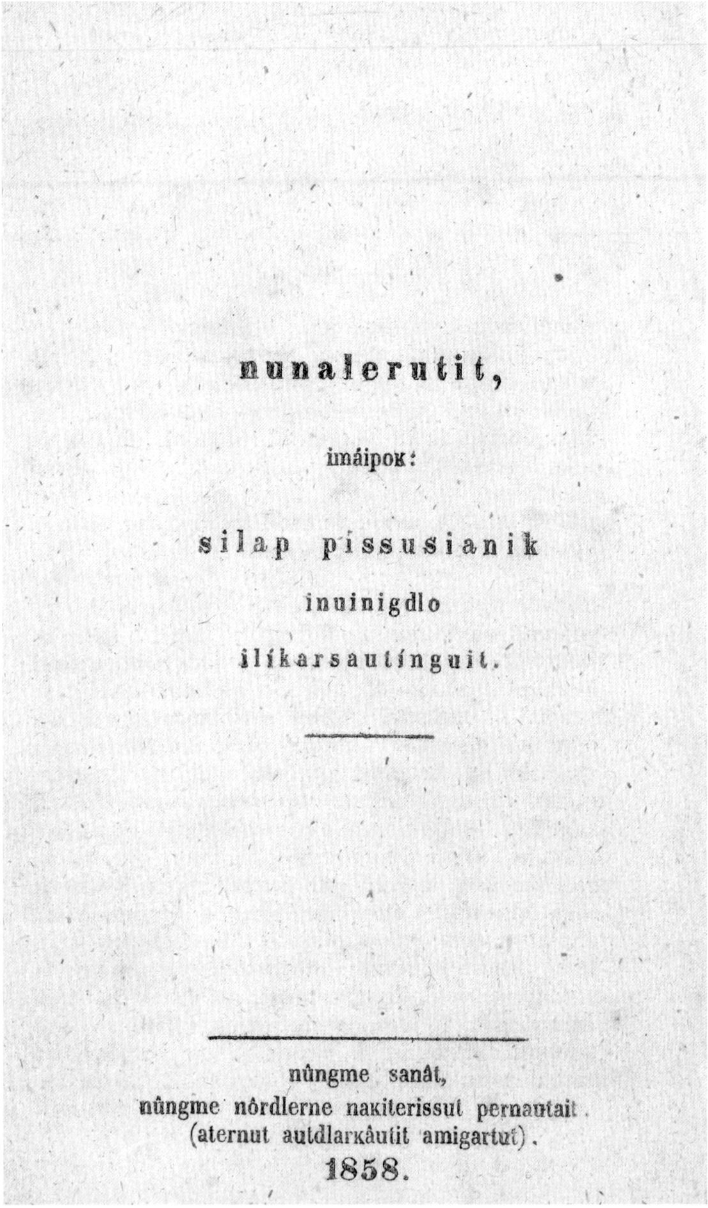

nunalerutit,

imáipoĸ:

silap pissusianik

inuinigdlo

ilíkarsautínguit.

nûngme sanât,
nûngme nôrdlerne naĸiterissut pernautait.
(aternut autdlarĸâutit amigartut).

1858.

FIGURE 9: *Nunalerutit* was the first publication Samuel Kleinschmidt produced on his printing press in Nuuk, in 1858.
SOURCE: KENN HARPER COLLECTION.

FIGURE 10: Mikak and her son Tutauk, painted by John Russell, 1769.
SOURCE: © ETHNOLOGISCHE SAMMLUNG DER GEORG-AUGUST-UNIVERSITÄT
GÖTTINGEN (BIKAT 26). PHOTOGRAPHER: HARRY HAASE.

FIGURE 14: Bishop John Horden, first bishop of Moosonee, photographed about 1872.

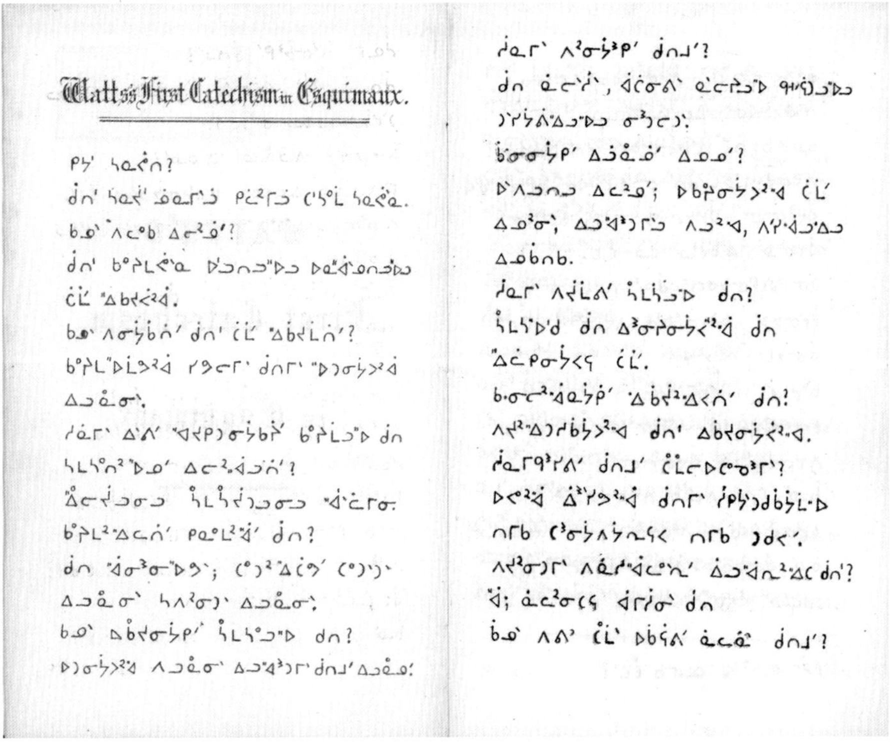

Watts's First Catechism in Esquimaux.

FIGURE 15: A page from *Watts's First Catechism in Esquimaux*, the second book ever printed in Inuktitut syllabics, in England, 1868 or 1869. Although the text is in Inuktitut, the final consonant symbols are those used for Cree.

FIGURE 16: Reverend Joseph Lofthouse in Inuit costume, about 1890.
SOURCE: JOSEPH LOFTHOUSE, *A THOUSAND MILES FROM A POST OFFICE*. LONDON:
SOCIETY FOR PROMOTING CHRISTIAN KNOWLEDGE, 1922. FRONTISPIECE. (KENN HARPER
COLLECTION.)

Bishop Lofthouse (Keewatin, Canada) addressing Eskimo.

FIGURE 17: Bishop Lofthouse preaching to Inuit in the Kivalliq region, circa 1900.
SOURCE: KENN HARPER COLLECTION.

FIGURE 18: Reverend Edmund Peck as a young man.
SOURCE: KENN HARPER COLLECTION.

FIGURE 19: Reverend Edmund Peck at Blacklead Island.
SOURCE: THE GENERAL SYNOD ARCHIVES, ANGLICAN CHURCH OF CANADA, P7502-45B.

FIGURE 20: Peck reads from a book while an Inuit man looks on.
SOURCE: THE GENERAL SYNOD ARCHIVES, ANGLICAN CHURCH OF CANADA, P7502-69.

FIGURE 21: Peck with Inuit at an outdoor prayer meeting on Blacklead Island.
SOURCE: THE GENERAL SYNOD ARCHIVES, ANGLICAN CHURCH OF CANADA, P7502-12.

FIGURE 22: The Church at Blacklead Island, drawn by an Inuk during Peck's time as missionary.

SOURCE: THE GENERAL SYNOD ARCHIVES, ANGLICAN CHURCH OF CANADA, PECK PAPERS, M 56-1, SERIES XXXIII, #8, REPRODUCED IN FRÉDÉRIC LAUGRAND, JARICH OOSTEN, AND MAKKI KAKKIK, *MEMORY AND HISTORY IN NUNAVUT, VOLUME 3: KEEPING THE FAITH*. IQALUIT: NUNAVUT ARCTIC COLLEGE, 2003. 166.

FIGURE 23: Blacklead Island whaling station in 1903.
SOURCE: ALBERT PETER LOW, GEOLOGICAL SURVEY OF CANADA, LAC PA-053579.

FIGURE 24: Reverend Peck at Blacklead Island with the first three Inuit Anglican converts.
SOURCE: THE GENERAL SYNOD ARCHIVES, ANGLICAN CHURCH OF CANADA, P7502-22.

FIGURE 25: Anglican missionary Julian Bilby in Arctic dress.
SOURCE: THE GENERAL SYNOD ARCHIVES, ANGLICAN CHURCH OF
CANADA, P9314-431.

FIGURE 26: Reverend E. W. T. Greenshield and his wife.

SOURCE: A. L. FLEMING, *PERILS OF THE POLAR PACK*. TORONTO: MISSIONARY SOCIETY OF THE CHURCH OF ENGLAND IN CANADA, 1932. (FACING PAGE 33.) (KENN HARPER COLLECTION.)

FIGURE 27: Reverend
E. W. T. Greenshield at
Blacklead Island.
SOURCE: THE GENERAL SYNOD
ARCHIVES, ANGLICAN CHURCH
OF CANADA, P7502-7C.

FIGURE 28: Reverend E. W. T. Greenshield (foreground) and trader Jay Jensen building the hospital at Blacklead Island.

SOURCE: THE GENERAL SYNOD ARCHIVES, ANGLICAN CHURCH OF CANADA, P7502-35.

FIGURE 29: Peter Tulugarjuaq was one of the first Inuit to become a catechist at Blacklead Island.

SOURCE: A POSTCARD IN THE *DWELLERS IN ARCTIC NIGHT* SERIES, PC5, KENN HARPER COLLECTION.

FIGURE 36: A drawing by Apak, daughter of the shaman Aua. In the centre is a four-legged mountain spirit that she saw one night.
SOURCE: KNUD RASMUSSEN, *INTELLECTUAL CULTURE OF THE IGLULIK ESKIMOS, REPORT OF THE FIFTH THULE EXPEDITION 1921–24*, VOLUME VII, NO. 1. COPENHAGEN: GYLDENDALSKE BOGHANDEL, 1929. (FACING PAGE 129.)

FIGURE 37: Helping spirits drawn by Unaleq.
SOURCE: KNUD RASMUSSEN, *INTELLECTUAL CULTURE OF THE IGLULIK ESKIMOS, REPORT OF THE FIFTH THULE EXPEDITION 1921–24*, VOLUME VII, NO. 1. COPENHAGEN: GYLDENDALSKE BOGHANDEL, 1929. (FACING PAGE 144.)

FIGURE 38: Unaleq, the shaman who drew his helping spirits, sketched by Kaj Birket-Smith on the Fifth Thule Expedition.
SOURCE: NATIONAL MUSEUM OF DENMARK, ETHNOGRAPHY DEPARTMENT, #533.

FIGURE 41: Bishop Isaac Stringer.
SOURCE: THE GENERAL SYNOD ARCHIVES, ANGLICAN CHURCH OF CANADA, P7565-75.

FIGURE 42: Inuit in front of the church at Lake Harbour.
SOURCE: THE GENERAL SYNOD ARCHIVES, ANGLICAN CHURCH OF CANADA, P9314-182.

FIGURE 43: Percy Broughton, missionary at Lake Harbour, taken circa 1912.
SOURCE: THE GENERAL SYNOD ARCHIVES, ANGLICAN CHURCH OF CANADA, P7502-29.

FIGURE 44: The headstone on the grave of Reverend Percy Broughton in Port Bickerton, Nova Scotia.
SOURCE: FIND A GRAVE, ONLINE, PHOTOGRAPHER UNKNOWN.

FIGURE 45: Father Turquetil was the first Roman Catholic bishop of the Arctic.
SOURCE: *ESKIMO MAGAZINE*, DECEMBER 1955, P. 4.

FIGURE 46: Akumalik, who brought Christianity from Cumberland Sound to the Pond Inlet area.
SOURCE: LACHLAN T. BURWASH / LIBRARY AND ARCHIVES CANADA / PA-099150.

FIGURE 47: Umik, who took his misunderstood version of Christianity to the Inuit of Igloolik.

SOURCE: PHOTOGRAPH BY THERKEL MATHIASSEN, NATIONAL MUSEUM OF DENMARK, ETHNOGRAPHY DEPARTMENT, #826.

FIGURE 48: Therkel Mathiassen from the Fifth Thule Expedition took this photograph of snow houses near Igloolik with flags flying above them. This was a sign that the occupants had adopted Christianity.

FIGURE 49: Canon William James teaching syllabics to Inuit children.

FIGURE 50: A manual keyboard in syllabics.
SOURCE: KENN HARPER COLLECTION.

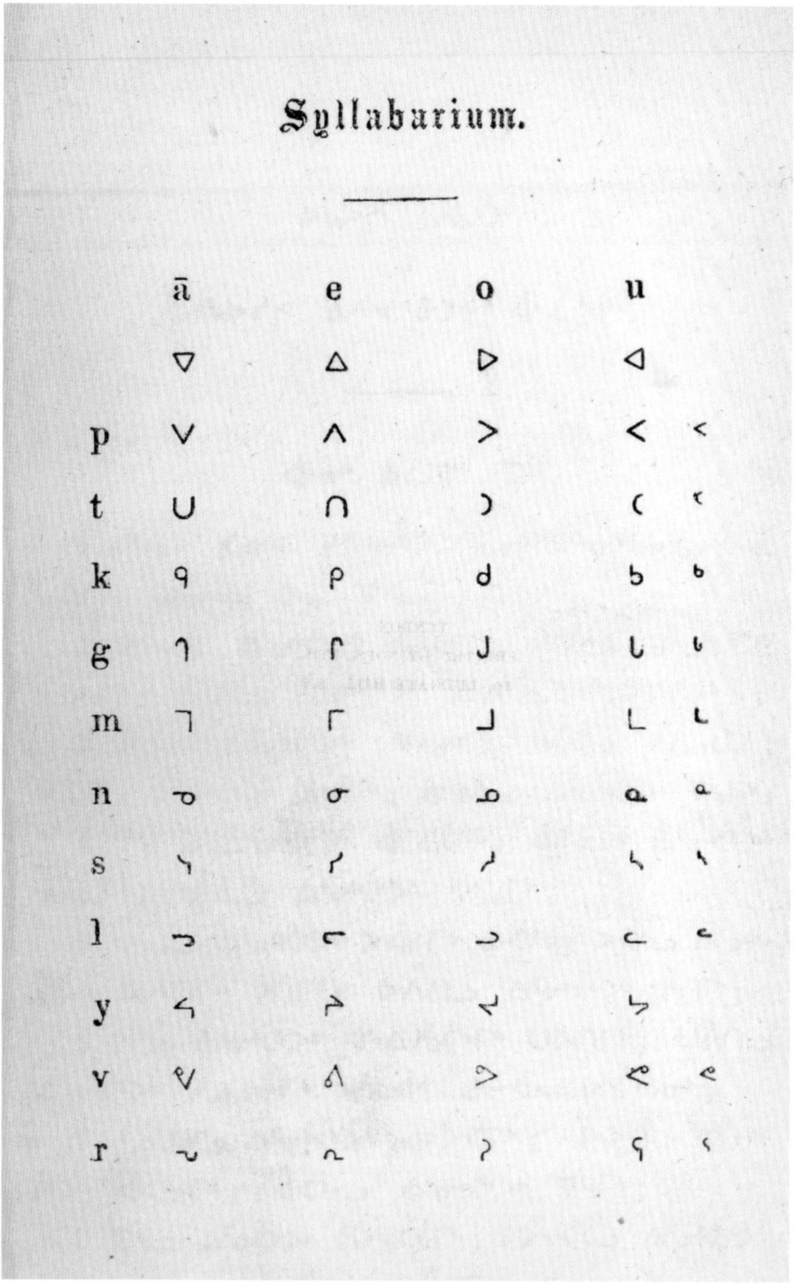

Syllabarium.

	ā	e	o	u	
	▽	△	▷	◁	
p	∨	∧	>	<	‹
t	∪	∩	)	(	⸦
k	٩	ρ	ᖱ	ᑫ	ᖯ
g	ᒉ	ᒉ	J	ᑐ	ᑐ
m	ᒣ	ᒥ	ᒧ	ᒪ	ᒪ
n	ᓄ	σ	ᓇ	ᓇ	ᓇ
s	ᔦ	ᔨ	ᔨ	ᔭ	ᔨ
l	ᓀ	ᑦ	ᒃ	ᒃ	ᒃ
y	ᔦ	ᐸ	ᐸ	ᐅ	
v	ᐁ	ᐱ	ᐳ	ᐊ	ᐊ
r	ᕒ	ᕒ	?	ᕐ	ᕐ

FIGURE 51: All Anglican Bibles used to have a syllabarium—a Syllabic chart—at the beginning. This is from a 1902 Bible.

SOURCE: KENN HARPER COLLECTION.

FIGURE 52: Orpingalik, Inuit poet.
SOURCE: KNUD RASMUSSEN, *THE NETSILIK ESKIMOS: SOCIAL LIFE AND SPIRITUAL CULTURE. REPORT OF THE FIFTH THULE EXPEDITION 1921–24*, VOLUME VIII, NO. 1&2. COPENHAGEN: GYLDENDALSKE BOGHANDEL, 1931. (FACING PAGE 29.)

FIGURE 53: The Catholic Mission tent in Arctic Bay, where the missionary lived until his mission was built.
SOURCE: KENN HARPER COLLECTION.

FIGURE 54: *The Flying Cross*, an airplane piloted by Father Paul Schulte on rescue missions.

FIGURE 55: Reverend (later Canon) John Hudspith Turner, who ministered in Pond Inlet and Moffet Inlet.

SOURCE: THE GENERAL SYNOD ARCHIVES, ANGLICAN CHURCH OF CANADA, P9314-93.

FIGURE 56: Peter Sala (left), one of the perpetrators of the Belcher Island murders in 1942.

SOURCE: FREDERICA KNIGHT FONDS, AVATAQ CULTURAL INSTITUTE, FK-011.

FIGURE 57: Mina, the sister of Peter Sala, was responsible for the deaths of a number of women and children during the Belcher Island murders.

SOURCE: FREDERICA KNIGHT FONDS, AVATAQ CULTURAL INSTITUTE, FK-009.

FIGURE 58: Reverend Donald Whitbread teaches Inuktitut using Syllabics to students in Frobisher Bay in June 1972.

FIGURE 59: Reverend Donald Whitbread, with wife Pat and children Heather, Aven, Martin, and Dhugal, in Frobisher Bay, circa 1970.

FIGURE 60: The inside front of Mary Cousins's copy of the Book of Genesis in Inuktitut.

SOURCE: KENN HARPER COLLECTION.

FIGURE 61: Mary Panigusiq (later to be Mary Cousins) and her father, Lazaroosie Kyak. Mary was a well-known teacher of Inuktitut.

SOURCE: KENN HARPER COLLECTION.

But it was not Greenshield's own arrival that caused a stir in the Granite City. It was his companion. For Greenshield was escorting Annie Sikuliaq to join her lover in England.

Earlier that year, Bilby had resigned from CMS. The society had probably asked for his resignation in light of his relationship with Annie. What they thought of Greenshield's agreement to escort her to Scotland is not recorded. Bilby awaited her arrival there.

In November Peck, the elder statesman of Arctic missionaries, wrote that "the Eskimo woman whom he [Bilby] had promised to marry has arrived safely with our brave young brother Greenshield. Mr. Bilby doubtless thinks as I do myself ... that our damp home climate would never suit her so he speaks of going to Canada."

Indeed, Bilby now had a more serious problem. Out of a job and with a fiancée to support, he needed to find work, and he wanted it to be as a missionary. Peck was an advocate for the young man and suggested that he write to the Bishop of Moosonee to ask for a position for himself and for Annie, whom he described as "a most intelligent and useful woman." Peck thought that the mission should find him work, "he having repented of his offence." It is not clear to what offence Peck was referring. He had violated mission policy by taking up with Annie. But the more serious crime, in Peck's view, was probably his offensive behaviour to the whalers.

And then Bilby confounded matters. Annie was in poor health. The climate of Norwich, where they lived with or near Bilby's mother, clearly did not agree with her. And the long-discussed marriage still had not happened. And then the unthinkable. The young couple decided not to marry after all. No one knows whose decision this was. It may well have been mutual.

In Those Days

Bilby's problem now was how to get Annie—who spoke no English—safely back to far-off Blacklead Island. He certainly could not simply send her alone as the only woman aboard a whaling ship. Crawford Noble was not sending a ship out in 1907, but a rival, Robert Kinnes of Dundee, was. But whaling was a tightly knit fraternity, and Kinnes undoubtedly knew the reputation that accompanied Bilby. He refused to allow passage for the missionary and Annie.

Somehow the two made it to Reykjavik. There they met, almost certainly by prearrangement, with a Scottish whaler that had been fishing off the east Greenland coast. The *Scotia* put in to port in the small Icelandic community on July 31 to take on coal and pick up mail destined for the *CGS Arctic*, a Canadian sovereignty vessel that had wintered in the High Arctic. Captain Tom Robertson—nicknamed "Coffee Tam" because of his adamant refusal to allow alcohol aboard any ship he commanded—took the star-crossed couple on board and left for Baffin Island on August 3. Bilby later praised him lavishly for his kindness.

The vessel reached the mouth of Cumberland Sound on the 17th of the month, but ice barred its passage, so Robertson set his course for Durban Island, Broughton Island, and Cape Hooper. At Hooper he learned from Inuit that the *Diana* had left the day before, having taken one small whale, but that the rest of the Scottish fleet was "clean"—whalers' parlance for not having taken any whales. Turning southward again, the *Scotia* finally reached Blacklead Island on September 1.

Bilby wrote, "After much trouble & expense & anxiety I have got my friend safely back again with her relatives. She is much stronger now and better than she was in England & her relatives are very pleased with the care that has been taken with her & the help given."

And then another problem. Captain Robertson had no room to take Bilby back to Scotland. The missionary would have to spend the winter in Cumberland Sound. But Robertson had only a minimum of stores that he could sell him. It was not appropriate for Bilby to stay on Blacklead Island, where Annie would live. Ironically, then, Bilby, who had railed against cooperation with traders, had to move in with the new agent that Robert Kinnes was setting up in Kekerten, assisting in the trade and doing whatever teaching he could. At the time Blacklead was home to 157 Inuit, Kekerten to 140.

In 1908 Reverend Greenshield travelled to Cumberland Sound on a Dundee vessel, the *Queen Bess*. He visited the Inuit on Blacklead, administered the sacraments to those who had been baptized, and found Bilby at Kekerten, willing to stay on for another year if he could get enough food. But the *Queen Bess* carried no extra supplies, so Bilby left for England with Greenshield.

Greenshield also learned something else at Blacklead Island. Annie Sikuliaq had passed away in November of 1907, less than three months after returning home. Writing of her, he said, "Our friend whom he [Bilby] was anxious to marry was called to her rest shortly before Xmas. The old trouble from which she was suffering in England re-asserted itself in an acute form, & the end came soon. I am led to believe that it was a triumphant death." This nonsense is missionary-speak for "she died a Christian."

Julian Bilby eventually reappeared as a missionary at Lake Harbour, and later in Bombay, India. He lived out his final days at a parish in England, where he died in 1932 at the age of 61. Presumably, his death too was "triumphant."

In Those Days

E. W. T. Greenshield: The Making of a Missionary

When John Horden, Bishop of Moosonee, put out a call for a young man to take up the post of missionary to the Inuit in lower Hudson Bay and James Bay in 1875, he wanted a practical man, preferably someone who had been a sailor. Edmund James Peck took up the challenge. When the Church Missionary Society interviewed him, they asked what climate he preferred. "Cold" was his one-word answer. He told them that he was "keenly desirous of being sent to the wildest and roughest mission-field in the world."

The CMS had been founded in 1799 as a conservative, evangelical movement within the Church of England. Its activities at first centred on Africa and China, but it extended its reach to other parts of the globe, including, eventually, the Arctic. The society operated its own theological college and a pre-college preparatory institute. The focus at these training institutions was on taking poorly educated young men with practical skills and training them in theology, Hebrew, Latin, Greek, and elementary medicine, as well as practical trades like printing, tinsmithing, blacksmithing, and carpentry.

The name of Peck is synonymous with early Arctic mission work, but if a second name were needed, it would surely be that of Reverend Edgar William Tyler Greenshield. He was born in 1877 in Newport on the Isle of Wight, off the southern coast of England. His father was a draper who was determined that his son would receive a good education. So young Edgar was sent to Portland House Academy, a local school designed to qualify boys for "commercial or professional life." The curriculum there was ambitious. Students got a thorough grounding in English, arithmetic, algebra, history, geography, scripture, languages, chemistry, shorthand, and bookkeeping. Greenshield received an all-round education there, but he excelled only at chemistry.

In 1895, when he was fifteen, Greenshield left school. Probably his family could no longer afford his tuition. Putting his practical skills to use, he went to work as a cabinetmaker, working for his uncle. At about the same time, he decided that he wanted to become a missionary.

When he was only four years old, his father had taken him to hear a talk given by John Horden, the same man who had called Peck to the mission field. The Bishop of Moosonee was on a tour in England, raising money to support his mission. After his lecture, Horden had placed his hand on young Greenshield's head and blessed him, praying that someday the boy would enter mission work. Greenshield always looked on that event as his calling to the field.

He applied to CMS for acceptance at the preparatory school, but was rebuffed because of his youth and lack of education. Determined, he went back to Portland House Academy, this time for night classes. In 1897 he reapplied to CMS and this time was accepted at the preparatory school. Two years later, he entered the theological college at Islington, a course designed to last three years.

Greenshield made it known that his heart was set on going to the Arctic, but CMS told him that there was little hope of this as the Society was not expanding its work there. Instead, he volunteered to go to Sierra Leone when his course of studies was finished. Then, unexpectedly, Edmund Peck appealed for a young man to go out to assist him on Blacklead Island. Greenshield still had a year to go to graduate, but he spontaneously answered Peck's call. On May 7, 1901, CMS accepted Greenshield as a missionary to the Inuit. Two months later he was heading north on the whaling vessel *Alert*, bound for Blacklead.

The wheel had come full circle. A four-year-old boy had been blessed by John Horden, the bishop who had called Edmund Peck to the mission field. Twenty years later, that young man was bound for the Arctic to join Edmund Peck. His association with Arctic missions would last for the next twelve years.

Inuit Catechists at Blacklead

It was always the goal of the Church Missionary Society that its missionaries at Blacklead Island would train a small cadre of Inuit catechists to carry on the work of the church when there were no missionaries at the station, and to advance the work of the mission into areas where white preachers had not ventured.

Tulugarjuaq was one such Inuit leader. He had been born in Cumberland Sound during the heyday of whaling activity, sometime around 1860, and achieved a position of importance in that industry in adulthood. He was not among Reverend Edmund Peck's earliest converts at the Blacklead Island mission, and, as an *angakkuq*—a shaman—he opposed the missionaries in the beginning. But, with one other man and five women, he converted to Christianity on February 9, 1902. His wife, Angalik, was known to be an *angakkuq* for some time after her husband's conversion. (There are various spellings of this man's name in church records, including Tooloakjuak and Tooloogarjuaq. I have used the modern spelling, Tulugarjuaq, throughout.)

Peck mentions Tulugarjuaq favourably in his journal in November 1903: "Had one of the men with me who has long been a subject of prayer." Peck invited him to become a teacher, to which the man readily agreed. He went on: "Tulugarjuaq— for this is the name of our friend—is one of the most promising candidates for baptism, has a good rapport amongst the Eskimo, and is in many ways, a very reliable man." Once he began leading prayer meetings that fall, men finally began attending evening services. Peck's fellow missionary, Julian Bilby, described him as "a quiet, pleasant man, and respected by his fellow men, both for his generosity in times of need and for his good hunting qualities."

The following Sunday, which Peck described effusively as "a day of days," Tulugarjuaq was appointed a teacher in front of a large congregation. He read a passage from the Bible in Inuktitut, after which Peck spoke to the people "of the necessity of teachers being raised up from their own people."

Tulugarjuaq was baptized on February 21, 1904. He read to the congregation from Acts 9, verses 1 to 10, and then spoke to the assemblage about St. Paul's conversion. Peck noted, "How the people did look and listen as he exhorted them to turn to Jesus. The whole service was one of power and blessing." One has to wonder what this little congregation on windswept Blacklead Island in mid-winter actually understood of the conversion of a man in a far-off Mediterranean country almost two thousand years earlier.

In addition to his role as a teacher among the Inuit, Tulugarjuaq remained active as a hunter, and became captain of a whaleboat later that year. But hunting trips were also occasions for ministry; as Bilby wrote: "While all the men were at the floeedge he held services for them." His name appears often in

In Those Days

Bilby's reports, and in those of Greenshield. In 1911 when Edgar Greenshield, the last Qallunaaq missionary to live at Blacklead, returned to the station, which had had no white missionary for a year, he wrote, "I found the church, house, hospital and store all in perfect order, they having been again taken care of by our Senior Native Teacher, Peter Tulugarjuaq."

With the mission closed and whaling at an end, Tulugarjuaq and his extended family left Blacklead Island in 1923 and settled at Qimmiqsut, in a camp that numbered about seventy people at its maximum. He was about sixty-five years of age, and his influence as a camp boss was beginning to wane. But he continued to preach. One elder recalled simply, "He converted many people to Christianity because he talked like a great preacher." Tulugarjuaq died at Qimmiqsut in the 1940s.

* * *

Another well-known catechist from Blacklead Island was Luke Killaapik (often written as Kidlapik). He is first mentioned in Peck's journal in April 1904 in a description of a disaster on the sea ice a month earlier. His prowess as a hunter was critical to the survival of the group.

The tragedy occurred when the ice on which a group of Inuit were camped began to break up. Three lives were lost. Killaapik managed to grab his gun, and his younger brother seized a number of cartridges. They and a few others made it to an uninhabited island close to Blacklead. There they killed four ptarmigans, and finally a seal. "Two of the party had been able to save their knives," wrote Reverend Peck. "With these poor tools they managed to … make three very small snow-houses. Into these they crept, and thus managed to shelter themselves from the piercing cold." Finally, someone on Blacklead spotted them with a telescope and sent a dog sled off over the newly formed ice. They were saved.

Killaapik was already a candidate for baptism at the time of his ordeal on the ice. His wife, Rhoda Sirmik, had been on the ice with him. The couple was baptized a few months later, on July 17.

Killaapik turns up occasionally in missionary journals and letters, although not with the frequency that Tulugarjuaq does. He travelled with Reverend Greenshield from the mission to other camps occasionally.

He was not averse to travelling far from home. He turns up at Lake Harbour (now Kimmirut) in 1912 and appears in the records there often. Peck, on a summer voyage, met him there in 1917. That year Killaapik ministered to the people at Lake Harbour until after Christmas, then embarked on a journey to Frobisher Bay, where he preached to about 120 Inuit. In 1919 he was working again in Lake Harbour, teaching the Inuit employed at the Scottish mica mine.

Reverend Archibald Lang Fleming, later Bishop of the Arctic, wrote about Killaapik in 1920: "He has gained for himself a position of greatest confidence and influence in the hearts and minds of the Eskimo and the HBC officers, all holding him in highest regard. His wife is a splendid helpmate."

Anglican church records contain letters from Killaapik to Peck and Greenshield. Usually these talk about the work he is doing among the Inuit and the poverty the people face. Often he asks for a little help from the missionaries: Could they send him a new rifle, some ammunition, a pocket knife, some tobacco? There is no way of knowing if all of his requests were met, but on one occasion Peck sent him a new rifle.

In Those Days

In 1924 Reverend Blevin Atkinson, missionary at Lake Harbour, visited the Inuit who had repopulated Southampton Island. They were from the Repulse Bay (now Naujaat) area and the south Baffin coast. The following year, those Inuit wrote to him asking for a permanent teacher. Atkinson sent Luke Killaapik and his wife. Killaapik spent a long and active ministry at Coral Harbour, and died there in 1954. *The Arctic News,* a publication of the Anglican Church, carried the following brief notice:

"It is with deepest regret that we record the loss of another link with the early days. This summer our faithful catechist, Luke Kidlapik [Killaapik], and his son died in an epidemic there [Southampton Island]. Luke was trained by Dr. E. J. Peck and Bishop Fleming, and spent thirty-five years in service for his Lord and Master among his own people. To his wife we extend our heartfelt sympathy."

There were other worthy teachers among the Inuit of Blacklead Island, including Aatami Naullaq (Adam Nowdlak). Fleming—not yet a bishop—met him near Lake Harbour in 1920 and described him as "a man of very sincere Christian character, and an excellent hunter." He noted further that "he is highly esteemed by the Eskimo wherever he goes, and ... preaches the Word very simply and effectively without remuneration from the Mission." That fall Naullaq left for Frobisher Bay on the Hudson's Bay Company's schooner *Nannuk,* intending to remain there as a hunter and a minister.

As Christianity spread among the Inuit, many teachers also came to prominence among Inuit who had not been taught at Blacklead. They continued the work begun by Tulugarjuaq, Killaapik, and Naullaq.

Becoming a Shaman

Igjugaarjuk Becomes a Shaman

In 1922 the ethnologist and explorer Knud Rasmussen travelled in the interior of the Kivalliq region and visited the Paallirmiut Inuit who lived on Lake Hikuligjuaq. There he met Igjugaarjuk, whom he described as an unusual man who enjoyed great esteem among his countrymen. Rasmussen had been told by other Inuit that Igjugaarjuk would be the ideal person to assist the traveller in understanding the customs of the Paallirmiut. Rasmussen wrote that the man was "wise, independent, intelligent and exercised great authority over his fellow-villagers."

Igjugaarjuk was a shaman and told his visitor about the spirits that governed the lives of the inland Inuit, those whom scientists called the "Caribou Eskimos." On the coast the Inuit feared Nuliajuk, the spirit called Sedna in some other parts of the North, who governed access to the animals of the sea. But inland Inuit, who depended almost entirely on the caribou for their survival, knew nothing of a spirit by that name, fearing instead one called Pinga—the one up in the sky—who was the guardian of all life, both animal and human. They also feared Hila, the spirit of the air.

Rasmussen was interested in how a man became a shaman and asked Igjugaarjuk to describe the training he had undergone. Igjugaarjuk told him that one could only become a shaman through sufferings that are almost enough to kill. Here is his story:

When I was to be a shaman, I chose suffering through the two things that are most dangerous to us humans, suffering through hunger and suffering through cold. First I hungered five days and was then allowed to drink a mouthful of warm water. The old ones say that only if the water is warm will Pinga and Hila notice the novice and help him. Thereafter I went hungry another fifteen days, and again was given a mouthful of warm water. After that I hungered for ten days, and then could begin to eat, though it only had to be ... the sort of food on which there is never any taboo, preferably fleshy meat.... I was to keep to this diet for five moons, and then the next five moons might eat anything. But after that I was again forced to eat the meat diet that is prescribed for all those who must do penance in order to become clean.

My instructor was my wife's father, Perqannaaq. When I was to be exhibited to Pinga and Hila, he dragged me on a little sledge that was no bigger than I could just sit on. He dragged me far over on the other side of Hikoligjuaq. It was a very long day's journey inland to a place we call Kingaarjuit—

the high hills.... It was in winter time and took place at night with the new moon. One could just see the very first streak of the moon; it had just appeared in the sky. I was not fetched again until the next moon was of the same size.

Perqannaaq built a small snow hut at the place where I was to be, this snow hut being no bigger than that I could just get under cover and sit down. I was given no sleeping skin to protect me against the cold, only a little piece of caribou skin to sit upon. There I was shut in.... When I had sat there for five days, Perqannaaq came with water, tepid, wrapped in caribou skin, a watertight caribou-skin bag. Not until fifteen days afterwards did he come again and hand me the same, just giving himself time to hand it to me, and then he was gone again, for even the old shaman must not interrupt my solitude....

Perqannaaq enjoined me to think of one single thing all the time I was to be there, to want only one single thing, and that was to draw Pinga's attention to the fact that there I sat and wished to be a shaman.

My novitiate took place in the middle of the coldest winter, and I ... was very cold, and it was so tiring having to sit without daring to lie down, that sometimes it was as if I died a little. Only towards the end of the thirty days did a helping spirit come to me, a lovely and beautiful helping spirit. It was a white woman. She came to me whilst I had collapsed, exhausted, and was sleeping. But still I saw her lifelike, hovering over me, and from that day I could not close my eyes or dream without seeing her. There is this remarkable thing about my helping spirit, that I have never seen her while awake, but only in dreams. She came to me

In Those Days

from Pinga and was a sign that Pinga had now noticed me and would give me powers that would make me a shaman.[1]

The beliefs of the inland Inuit in the Kivalliq, the so-called Caribou Eskimos, were quite different than those of Inuit on the coast. Whereas the Inuit of the coast believed that a shaman could summon seals by placating the woman of the sea, the inland Inuit believed that the animals had definite laws for their own wanderings, laws with which no shaman could interfere.

Igjugaarjuk believed that true wisdom could only be attained "through sufferings in solitude of almost sublime simplicity."

After Igjugaarjuk had endured the time of privation on the land, which prepared him for his role as a shaman, his teacher, Perqannaaq, came to fetch him "when a new moon was lighted and had the same size as the one that had shone for us when we left the village." The older man hauled him home on his sled, for the newly trained shaman was too weak to stand. He had slowly to be nursed back to health.

Igjugaarjuk resumed his story:

> Later, when I had become quite myself again, I understood that I had become the shaman of my village, and it did happen that my neighbours or people from a long distance away called me to heal a sick person, or to inspect a course if they were going to travel. When this happened, the people of my village were called together and I told them what I had been

---

[1] Knud Rasmussen, *Intellectual Culture of the Caribou Eskimos. Report of the Fifth Thule Expedition 1921-24*, Vol. VII, No. 2 (Copenhagen: Gyldendalske Boghandel, 1930), 52–53.

asked to do. Then I left the tent or snowhouse and went out into solitude: *ahiarmut*, away from the dwellings of man....

If anything difficult had to be found out, my solitude had to extend over three days and two nights, or three nights and two days. In all that time I had to wander about without rest, and only sit down once in a while on a stone or a snow drift. When I had been out long and had become tired, I could almost doze and dream what I had come out to find and about which I had been thinking all the time. Every morning, however, I could come home and report on what I had so far found, but as soon as I had spoken I had to return again, out into the open, out to places where I could be quite alone....

These days of seeking for knowledge are very tiring, for one must walk all the time, no matter what the weather is like and only rest in short snatches. I am usually quite done up, tired, not only in body but also in head, when I have found what I sought.

We shamans in the interior have no special spirit language, and believe that the real *angakkut* do not need it.[2]

Igjugaarjuk took a dim view of the practices of shamans on the sea coast. He told Knud Rasmussen:

These *angakkut* never seemed trustworthy to me. It always appeared to me that these salt-water *angakkut* attached more weight to tricks that would astonish the audience, when they jumped about the floor and lisped all sorts of absurdities and lies in their so-called spirit language. To me

---

[2] Ibid., 53–54.

all this seemed only amusing and as something that would impress the ignorant. A real shaman does not jump about the floor and do tricks, nor does he seek by the aid of darkness, by putting out the lamps, to make the minds of his neighbours uneasy.

For myself, I do not think I know much, but I do not think that wisdom or knowledge about things that are hidden can be sought in that manner. True wisdom is only to be found far away from people, out in the great solitude, and it is not found in play but only through suffering. Solitude and suffering open the human mind, and therefore a shaman must seek his wisdom there.[3]

Another man from Hikuligjuaq, named Utahania, seems to have had a different opinion. He had criticized the abilities of one of the saltwater shamans, a man who was, however, highly respected among his own people. The offended shaman invited Utahania to attend a performance where he could demonstrate his prowess. Another Inuk who was present recounted what transpired there:

First the shaman shot himself in the forehead with a gun of heavy calibre. The bullet went in through his brow and came out through one sleeve. He shot himself in the heart in the same manner. Then he went out with the men of his village, while the women had to remain in the house. A shotgun was set up with the muzzle pointing towards him, and then he ran towards it and disappeared into the barrel. He could be heard speaking inside it. Then the shotgun

---

[3] Ibid., 54–55.

was carried into the house. It was then very heavy to carry. Inside the house they suddenly heard a voice from inside the barrel say "ipiliqihunga—I am choking." And so the gun was taken outside and the shaman crept out again.

This shaman had a walrus for an amulet, and he allowed his amulet to come into the entrance passage of the house. It could be heard dragging its heavy body in through the passage, and from the passage it squirted salt water in on to the floor of the house, for the shaman kept the walrus out in the passage and did not allow it to come inside. Later the walrus appeared at the window and the shaman harpooned it from the house through the window, without the window being broken. In this manner he convinced Utahania of his powers as a shaman, and after that Utahania declared himself a believer.[4]

The Inuk who recounted this story in 1922 was a skilled hunter, lively and curious about anything that was a little out of the ordinary. He maintained a healthy skepticism, feeling that there was as much reason to believe in the coastal shamans as to doubt them. "There are certainly *angakkut* who are frauds," he stated, then added, "but there are others, *qanukiaq*—I wonder..."

Kiinaalik Becomes a Shaman

Kiinaalik was a woman of about thirty years when the ethnographer Knud Rasmussen met her in the Kivalliq region in the 1920s.

---

[4] Ibid., 58–59.

In Those Days

He described her as intelligent, pleasant, and easy to talk with. Moreover, she was neat and clean, amiable and trustworthy.

She had a reputation among her people for being a powerful shaman. Like the male shamans in her group, she had a special shaman's belt, to which were attached a number of items used as amulets: part of a gun butt, a piece of sinew, a piece of ribbon that had been tied around a gift of tobacco, a piece of the cap of her deceased brother, a piece of white caribou skin, a piece of a knitted vest that had belonged to a white man, a caribou tooth, caribou-skin mittens, and part of the skin from a seal flipper. All of these items had been gifts and, as such, imparted magical powers to her.

Kiinaalik was the sister-in-law of the well-known shaman Igjugaarjuk. It became apparent to the people of her village that Kiinaalik was destined to become a shaman because of powerful dreams that she had had. She spent five days out in extreme weather, suspended from tent-poles above the ground, so that Hila—the weather spirit—might take notice of her. She felt no cold, because of the presence of her helping spirits. Next the people of her village were called together, and her mother, Abgaarjuk, decided that she should be shot, as this was also a means of acquiring shamanic power.

She sat in the snow house, in a kitchen off the entrance passage. Her brother-in-law, Igjugaarjuk, shot her with a small, round stone, and Kiinaalik fell over dead. The villagers held a song-feast while the woman lay dead the whole night. The next morning she woke up of her own accord. She had been shot through the heart—the stone was removed, and her mother preserved it.

This death and resurrection had made Kiinaalik acceptable to the spirits. Hila had noticed her, and helping spirits would henceforth come to her of their own volition. Chief among them was her dead brother, of whom she spoke freely and cheerfully, for among her people there was no prohibition on mentioning the names of the dead, as there was among the coast dwellers. Her brother "used to come to her gliding through the air, legs uppermost, head downwards, but as soon as he had reached the ground he could walk like an ordinary man."

She also had a polar bear as a helping spirit.

Igjugaarjuk trained her in shamanism, but he did not carry her training as far as he might, for he took pity on her suffering. Rasmussen, who learned all this from Igjugaarjuk, concluded that "the fact is that the more one suffers for one's art, the greater shaman one becomes."

Another method of becoming a shaman among the Caribou Inuit was to experience drowning. Rasmussen described this method in the training of a young man:

> Aggiaartoq was tied fast to a long tent pole and then carried by Igjugaarjuk and Ulibvaq—an elderly man in the village— down to a big lake. There a hole was hewn in the ice and, clad in caribou-skin frock, mittens and full outfit, Aggiaartoq, bound to the tent pole, was pushed down through the hole so that he stood on the bottom of the lake. There they let him stay five whole days, and when they took him up again he was as dry as if he had never been in the water. This young man's helping spirits were the spirit of his dead mother and a human skeleton.[5]

---

[5] Ibid., 58.

In Those Days

Niviatsian Becomes a Shaman

In the early 1920s, the explorer Knud Rasmussen travelled in northern Canada on his most famous expedition, the Fifth Thule Expedition. In the Iglulik area, Knud Rasmussen interviewed a well-known Inuk, Aua, and heard from him the story of how his cousin, Niviatsian, acquired his legendary shamanic powers. Here is Aua's story:

> Niviatsian was out hunting walrus with a number of other men near Iglulik; some were in front of him and others behind. Suddenly a great walrus came up through the ice close beside him, grasped him with his huge fore-flippers, just as a mother picks up her little child, and carried him off with it down into the deep. The other men ran up, and looking down through the hole in the ice where the walrus had disappeared, they could see it still holding him fast and trying to pierce him with its tusks. After a little while it let him go, and rose to the surface, a great distance off, to breathe. But Niviatsian, who had been dragged away from the hole through which he had first been pulled down, struggled with arms and legs to come up again. The men could follow his movements, and cut a hole about where they expected him to come up, and here my father actually did manage to pull him up. There was a gaping wound over his collarbone, and he was breathing through it; the gash had penetrated to the lung. Some of his ribs were broken, and the broken ends had caught in one of his lungs, so that he could not stand upright.
>
> Niviatsian lay for a long time unconscious. When he came to himself, however, he was able to get on his feet without

help. The wound over the collarbone was the only serious one; there were traces of the walrus's tusks both on his head and in different parts of his body, but it seemed as if the animal had been unable to wound him there. Old folk said that this walrus had been sent by the Mother of the Sea Beasts, who was angry because Niviatsian's wife had had a miscarriage and concealed the fact in order to avoid the taboo.

Niviatsian then went with his companions in towards land, but he had to walk a little way apart from them, on ice free from footmarks. Close to land, a small snow hut was built, and he was shut in there, laid down on a sealskin with all his wet clothes on. There he remained for three days and three nights without food or drink. This he was obliged to do in order to be allowed to live, for if he had gone up at once to the unclean dwellings of men after the ill-treatment he had received, he would have died.

All the time Niviatsian was in the little snow hut, the shaman up at the village was occupied incessantly in purifying his wife and his old mother, who were obliged to confess in the presence of others all their breaches of taboo, in order to appease the powers that ruled over life and death. And after three days, Niviatsian recovered, and had now become a great shaman. The walrus, which had failed to kill him, became his first helping spirit. That was the beginning.

Another time he was out hunting, it was on a caribou hunt up inland, he ran right up against a wolverine's lair. The animal had young ones, and attacked him furiously. It "wrestled" with him all day and night and did not leave hold of him until the sun was in the same place as when it had begun. But in spite of the animal's sharp teeth and claws, there was not a single wound on his body, only a few abrasions. Thus the wolverine also became his helping spirit.

His third helping spirit was Amajorjuk, the ogress with the great amaut on her back, in which she puts the human beings she carries off. She attacked him so suddenly, that he was in the bag already before he could think of doing anything. The bag closed over him at once, and he was shut in. But he had his knife round his neck, and with this he stabbed the woman in the back, just behind the shoulderblade, and she died. The amaut was as thick as walrus hide, and it took him a long time to cut his way out and escape. But now he discovered that he was altogether naked; he had no idea when he had been stripped of his clothes, nor did he know where he now was, save that it must be far, far inland. Not until he came down close to the sea did he find his clothes, and then he got safely home. But there was a horrible smell of rotten seaweed all over his body, and the smell hung about his house so obstinately that it was half a year before it went away. This ogress also became his helping spirit, and he was now regarded as the greatest of shamans among mankind.[6]

The Wisdom of Aua

It was February 1922. Knud Rasmussen was travelling by sled with his Polar Inuit companions along the shores of Foxe Basin,

---

[6] Knud Rasmussen, *Intellectual Culture of the Iglulik Eskimos. Report of the Fifth Thule Expedition 1921-24*, Vol. VII, No. 1 (Copenhagen: Gyldendalske Boghandel, 1929), 120–21.

north of Lyon Inlet. They were about to make camp for the night when suddenly, out of the darkness, appeared a team of fifteen white dogs pulling a long sled carrying six men. Sighting the party of strangers, a small man with a long beard, his face framed in ice and snow, leapt from the sled and ran towards Rasmussen. This, wrote Rasmussen, was Aua, the shaman.

Rasmussen's mission was to study and record the myths and legends, the beliefs and the life stories of the Inuit of Canada, who had had little contact with outsiders. He spoke Greenlandic fluently, and so he was easily able to understand the dialects he encountered on his sled-quest across Canada's North. He had heard of Aua from Inuit he had already met in Foxe Basin and was overjoyed to finally meet him. From Aua, his garrulous wife Orulo, and the others who lived in Aua's camp, Rasmussen learned much about the customs of the Inuit.

Through several evenings of discussions with the men of the camp about the rules and taboos that governed life, it was apparent that everyone knew what had to be done in any given situation. But Rasmussen wanted to know more. He wanted to know why. And to this simple question, he wrote, they could give no answer. "They regarded it as unreasonable," he added, "that I should require not only an account, but also a justification, of their religious principles."

One evening, unable to answer the repeated question of "why," Aua rose suddenly and invited Rasmussen to follow him outside, where a storm raged. He pointed to the ice and calmly remarked:

"In order to hunt well and live happily, man must have calm weather. Why this constant succession of blizzards and all this needless hardship for men seeking food for themselves and those they care for? Why? Why?"

In Those Days

By chance, hunters were returning from an unsuccessful day of hunting for seals at the breathing holes on the ice. Their efforts had been in vain, and Aua, turning the tables again, asked his companion, "Why?" Rasmussen could give no answer.

Aua led him to Kublo's snow house, where the *qulliq* gave barely enough light and offered no heat to the children shivering under a skin blanket.

"Why should it be cold and comfortless in here?" the shaman asked. "Kublo has been out hunting all day, and if he had got a seal, as he deserved, his wife would now be sitting laughing beside her lamp, letting it burn full, without fear of having no blubber left for tomorrow. The place would be warm and bright and cheerful, the children would come out from under their rugs and enjoy life. Why should it not be so? Why?"

They continued to the house of Aua's sister, Natseq, where Aua again questioned his questioner:

"Why must people be ill and suffer pain? We are all afraid of illness. Here is this old sister of mine; as far as anyone can see, she has done no evil; she has lived through a long life and given birth to healthy children, and now she must suffer before her days end. Why? Why?"

Silently they returned to Aua's snow house and resumed their conversation. Aua began:

You see. You are equally unable to give any reason when we ask you why life is as it is. And so it must be. All our customs come from life and turn towards life. We explain nothing, we believe nothing. But in what I have just shown you lies our answer to all you ask.

We fear the weather spirit of earth, that we must fight

against to wrest our food from land and sea. We fear Sila.

We fear dearth and hunger in the cold snow huts.

We fear Takannakapsaaluk, the great woman down at the bottom of the sea, that rules over all the beasts of the sea.

We fear the sickness that we meet with daily all around us; not death, but the suffering. We fear the evil spirits of life, those of the air, of the sea and the earth, that can help wicked shamans to harm their fellow men.

We fear the souls of dead human beings and of the animals we have killed.

Therefore it is that our fathers have inherited from their fathers all the old rules of life which are based on the experience and wisdom of generations. We do not know how, we cannot say why, but we keep those rules in order that we may live untroubled. And so ignorant are we in spite of all our shamans, that we fear everything unfamiliar. We fear what we see about us, and we fear all the invisible things that are likewise about us, all that we have heard of in our forefathers' stories and myths. Therefore we have our customs, which are not the same as those of the white men, the white men who live in another land and have need of other ways.[7]

This was Aua's explanation. Clearly and calmly, he had outlined to Rasmussen why his question of "why" must remain an enigma.

In his questioning of Aua, Rasmussen asked about Inuit religious ideas, and in particular about the soul. Aua replied:

---

[7] Ibid., 55–56.

In Those Days

We ignorant Eskimos living up here do not believe, as you have told us many white men do, in one great solitary spirit that from a place far up in the sky maintains humanity and all the life of nature. Among us, as I have already explained to you, all is bound up with the earth we live on and our life here; and it would be even more incomprehensible, even more unreasonable, if, after a life short or long, of happy days or of suffering and misery, we were then to cease altogether from existence. What we have heard about the soul shows us that the life of men and beasts does not end with death. When at the end of life we draw our last breath, that is not the end. We awake to consciousness again, we come to life again, and all this is effected through the medium of the soul. Therefore it is that we regard the soul as the greatest and most incomprehensible of all.[8]

Aua explained that most shamans divide the soul into two parts. These were, he said, *"inuusia,* of which we say that it is one with the spirit of life, and the spirit of life is something a living human being cannot do without. The other part of the soul is *tarninga,* perhaps the most powerful part of the soul, and the most mysterious, for while *tarninga* gives life and health, it is at the same time the site of disease, or the spot where any sickness enters in."

He recounted to Rasmussen the Inuit belief that in the very earliest times, there was no death among human beings. But the island on which they lived, said by some to be the island of Mitligjuaq in Hudson Strait, became so overpopulated that

---

[8] Ibid., 60.

eventually an old woman, with power in her words, began to shout, asking that human beings be able to die, or soon there would be no room left for them on earth.

Aua continued:

Mysterious as the manner in which death came into life, even so mysterious is death itself.

We know nothing about it for certain, save that those we live with suddenly pass away from us, some in a natural and understandable way because they have grown old and weary, others, however, in mysterious wise, because we who lived with them could see no reason why they in particular should die, and because we knew that they would gladly live. But that is just what makes death the great power it is. Death alone determines how long we may remain in this life on earth, which we cling to, and it alone carries us into another life which we know only from the accounts of shamans long since dead.

We know that men perish through age, or illness, or accident, or because another has taken their life. All this we understand. Something is broken. What we do not understand is the change which takes place in a body when death lays hold of it. It is the same body that went about among us and was living and warm and spoke as we do ourselves, but it has suddenly been robbed of a power, for lack of which it becomes cold and stiff and putrifies. Therefore we say that a man is ill when he has lost a part of his soul, or one of his souls, for there are some who believe that man has several souls. If then that part of a man's vital force be not restored to the body, he must die. Therefore we say that a man dies when the soul leaves him.[9]

Aua pointed out to his questioner that it was somewhat unusual to be asked to think about these things, and that usually such subjects were far from people's minds. "In our ordinary everyday life we do not think much about all these things," he explained, "and it is only now you ask that so many thoughts arise in my head of long-known things; old thoughts, but as it were becoming altogether new when one has to put them into words."

Aua Meets the Holy Ghost

Peter Freuchen, the great Danish explorer, travelled extensively with the Inuit of the Iglulik area in the early 1920s as part of the Fifth Thule Expedition. He was an avid student of Inuit life and would go on to write a number of books about his time in the North.

At first, he noted, the Inuit strictly observed the taboos that had been part of their traditional beliefs, what Freuchen called "their ancient pagan rules." This made life difficult for both the Inuit and the expedition members. Women could not sew caribou skins while the daylight hours were on the wane in the fall, and so the Danes had a difficult time getting local clothing made or repaired. Women could not eat from the same pot as the men while they were pregnant, and so extra time was spent in preparing meals. So many rules made life tedious.

---

[9] Ibid., 92–93.

"Then one day," wrote Freuchen,

> a man named Kutlok ("The Thumb") [Rasmussen spelled his name *Kublo*] returned from the south, where he had gone to deliver a letter. The man to whom the letter was addressed had moved, it seemed, and Kutlok had spent more than two years completing his mission. While in the south he had visited a school and received a taste of the Christian code of morals....
>
> So he became a teacher. In a short time he had won over all his people to Christianity. The conversions took place at a meeting, and immediately all the old restrictions fell by the wayside. In fact, it was a great relief to the natives to be able to sew all sorts of skins at any time of day or night, to be permitted to hunt whichever animals they needed.[10]

Freuchen was a keen observer of social and cultural change, and the conversion to Christianity afforded him a unique opportunity to observe the changes that the new belief brought. Although he was a lifelong atheist, he thought that Christianity served the Inuit well by freeing them from their oppressive taboos.

"There were a number of beliefs and rules which it was difficult for them to grasp," he wrote. "It was said that the missionaries did not favour wife-trading, and that would have to be stopped. However, so as not to make it too dull for the poor ladies, it was decided that Kutlok and a few of the mightiest men of the tribe should have the privilege of entertaining the girls, as it was

---

[10] Peter Freuchen, *Arctic Adventure: My Life in the Frozen North* (London & Toronto: William Heinemann Ltd., 1956), 341.

considered healthy for the women themselves and also for the children they would bear."

Some time later, Freuchen had occasion to travel with Aua, his wife, and their adopted son. Aua had been a powerful shaman, but he, too, was trying to understand the new beliefs that were quickly changing his society. The Inuit had of course heard of the Qallunaat missionaries who had taught the Inuit at Black-lead Island in southeast Baffin Island and of other missionaries at Chesterfield Inlet who believed in the same God but who followed somewhat different practices. Some Inuit had learned to read in Syllabics, even though there were no missionaries to explain to them what it was they were reading. And so they struggled with homemade interpretations of the new beliefs.

Just the previous summer, Aua told the Dane, he had had a remarkable experience. Freuchen commented that it "might have been even more remarkable if it had not been for a little girl who laughed at the wrong time":

He was sitting outside his tent carving a walrus tusk when he saw three men approaching the settlement. He did not know who they might be, but suddenly recognized them as the new gods of the trinity, the Father, the Son and the Holy Ghost.

Aua shouted for everyone to come out and receive the dignified guests. And then, when a certain little girl discovered they wore trousers of rabbit-skin and very tall caps, she had to laugh.

This made the Trinity angry, and, while they smiled forgivingly, they altered their course so that they passed by without stopping or even speaking a word in greeting. The natives had been greatly disappointed, but they said the Holy Ghost presented such a laughable aspect from the rear that they all gave way to their mirth. His posteriors curved in instead of out.[11]

And that was it—a confusing vision that Aua and his camp-mates saw, or thought they saw, at a time of intense cultural change and confusion.

The Trinity, Freuchen noted, were never seen again.

---

[11] Ibid.

Isaac Stringer

The Bishop Who Ate His Boots

While Church Missionary Society preachers were bringing the gospel to Inuit at a whaling station on Baffin Island, a similar scenario unfolded at the opposite end of the Arctic. The situation at Herschel Island, north of the Yukon mainland, roughly mirrored that at Blacklead Island. Both were populated by foreign whalemen—in Herschel Island's case mostly American rather than Scottish, but with a liberal admixture of Scandinavians, Polynesians, and immigrant Alaskan Inuit. The mission station depended on the whalers for accommodation and transportation.

Isaac Stringer was born on an Ontario farm in 1866. He attended Wycliffe College, a theological school associated with the University of Toronto. Once he accepted the call to Northern service, he took additional courses in medicine and dentistry.

His first posting, in 1892, was to Fort McPherson, where he was fortunate to serve under the veteran archdeacon Robert McDonald. But he knew from the outset that his calling was to serve the Inuit. In August of that year he visited Inuit on the coast for two weeks.

The following autumn he began a long journey, which took him for the first time to Herschel Island, from where he returned in the summer of 1894. Four whaling ships were frozen in at the island that winter. That summer Bishop Reeve ordained Stringer as a priest. The following year he and a new missionary, Reverend Charles Edward Whittaker, travelled with the bishop back to Herschel Island, and from there Stringer took a whaling ship to San Francisco for a one-year furlough.

In March of 1896 he married Sadie Alexander, an Ontario girl who had long been his fiancée. She had worked as a secretary in a New York law firm but had given that up to return to Canada and study nursing to better prepare herself to be the wife of a missionary.

The couple moved to Fort McPherson that summer, where their first child was born. In 1897 they moved to Herschel Island, where a second child arrived three years later. Isaac and Sadie were very much a team. Walter Vanast, a medical historian who has written about them, claims that the most repeated words in Isaac's diary were "my wife and I." Except when he was away on trips to visit Inuit, the pair were inseparable—on social calls, sick visitations, long walks together, and evenings spent reading. In addition to her household duties, Sadie taught classes for the Inuit and evening courses for the whalers. When Isaac was ill—which was often—she led church services.

The Stringers remained at Herschel Island until 1901. In that time, although the couple was very popular with the Inuit and

In Those Days

Isaac's worship services were well attended, he made not one single convert to Christianity. It was a measure of his honesty that he would not baptize people who were not ready just to pad the numbers.

Isaac had attained proficiency in the Inuit language and had translated hymns and prayers. He had hoped that teaching the Inuit to read would lead to more understanding and the eradication of pagan beliefs. But the opposite happened. The Bible became an object of awe, and written words were treated as amulets. Onc man, Avumnuk, asked the missionary to write the word for *seal* on a piece of paper. Isaac complied, then was horrified when he learned that the man wanted it "as a charm to put on his net so that he might get more seals." Others reasoned that, with a book as powerful as the Bible and with his medical skills, Isaac should be able to "work the book" and pray to God to cause the death of an unpopular man.

Their dependence on the whalers troubled Isaac. The mission house belonged to the whaling company. Their supplies came by whaling ship. Sadie's uncle acted as a trader for a whaling company, and Isaac was caretaker of their buildings in their absence. Many of the whalers used alcohol to excess and traded it to the Inuit for furs. Many Inuit loaned their wives to whalers in return for alcohol or other supplies. But, to the end of his stay, Isaac found no way out of this dependence.

In the summer of 1901 the Stringers took passage on a whaling ship to San Francisco. Isaac's health would not permit a return to Herschel Island. Their residency among the Inuit was at an end. Vanast has written, "It would be hard to imagine a brighter, more capable pair of southerners for the job. Yet they had not gained a single convert."

Isaac accepted the rectorship of the Anglican church in White-horse in 1903—for a time Robert Service was his vestry clerk. Two years later he was made Bishop of Selkirk, the Yukon diocese that had been created in 1891. (Its name was changed to Diocese of Yukon in 1907.) The previous bishop, Bompas, conveniently died in 1906, making the Episcopal Palace at Carcross (then called Cariboo Crossing) available for the Stringers. They didn't remain long there, however, moving to Dawson in 1907 when it was desig-nated the seat of the diocese. (At that time, Dawson was Yukon's capital and administrative centre.) They lived there until 1931.

In 1909, accompanied by Reverend Whittaker, Stringer trav-elled to the Arctic coast. There he baptized nine Inuit. Finally, his efforts had borne fruit.

But on that trip he very nearly lost his life. Returning from the coast, overland to Dawson, the party ran out of food. His diary entry for October 21 reads: "Breakfast of sealskin boot, soles and tops boiled and toasted. Soles better than uppers. Soup of small scraps of bacon and spoonful of flour (the scrapings of the flour bag), the last we had; tired; hands sore; took a long time to pack up." And then later in the day: "Heard children's voices in the distance and then saw houses on left hand about a mile ahead. We stopped and thanked God for bringing us in sight of human habitation."

Like most missionaries, Stringer was an able publicist—it helped in raising funds. When his brush with death reached the outside world, he became known as "the Bishop who ate his boots."

In 1931 Stringer became Archbishop of Rupert's Land and moved to Winnipeg. He died there three years later. Sadie lived until 1955.

A Church for
Lake Harbour

When the Church Missionary Society closed its station at Blacklead Island in 1906, the religious needs of the Inuit in southern Baffin Island were left in the hands of local men trained by Reverends Peck, Bilby, and Greenshield.

Then in 1909 the Anglican Church decided to open a mission at Lake Harbour, now Kimmirut, on the south coast of Baffin Island, in Hudson Strait. A small vessel, the *Lorna Doone*, was chartered in St. John's to carry supplies for a four-room mission house and the necessities of life for two years. Reverend Peck, now superintendent of the church's Arctic mission, accompanied the two missionaries who would remain at Lake Harbour: the veteran, Julian Bilby, and the newcomer, Archibald Lang Fleming.

As at Blacklead Island, so too at Lake Harbour, the missionaries

were not the first white men there. The Inuit of the Baffin coast of
Hudson Strait had traded with Hudson's Bay Company ships bound
farther west for well over a century. A Scottish whaling enterprise,
Robert Kinnes and Company, had a mica mine near Lake Harbour
at which both Inuit and white men were employed. In addition,
about eighty Inuit worked seasonally in Kinnes's whaling operation. Moreover, some of the Inuit had been to the Blacklead mission and had heard the gospel there. Nonetheless, Bilby and Fleming would be the first trained missionaries to live among them.

The first church service conducted at Lake Harbour was an
open-air one that Peck held on Sunday, August 29, shortly after
the missionaries' arrival, "under the shadow of a rocky cliff."

With the ship still in harbour, the missionaries and their Inuit
helpers quickly erected the dwelling that would be the missionaries' home. Putting up the shell of the building took a week, so
that on the following Sunday, September 5, they were able to hold
their service inside the cramped dwelling. "Thus was it dedicated
to the service of God," wrote Fleming. But it still wasn't a church.
That would have to wait.

After a few years it was decided to modify a small storehouse by
removing one end and adding to that open end a second building,
the frame of which had been prefabricated in St. John's in 1909 but
had not been sent up until 1912. Bilby erected the frame. Then
both buildings, now one, had to be completely renovated. Fleming
noted, "The result of our work really seems quite satisfactory, and
we are justly proud of the little building when we compare it with
the places in which we have hitherto had to hold our services."

In September of 1913, with the church still not quite ready for
use, Bilby departed Lake Harbour aboard the ship *Pelican*, leaving Fleming to finish the building and continue missionary work

alone. The next year, in his annual letter, he wrote about the first service held in the new church: "On Sunday, 21st December, 1913, the little church at Lake Harbour was formally opened. It was far from being complete, but the intense cold had made it impossible to do anything more to it for the present. In the morning we had a joint service for white men and Eskimo, when everyone turned out."

He continued in the deprecating tone that missionaries often adopted in letters to their far-off supporters: "It was most interesting to see the extraordinary decorum with which the Eskimo conducted themselves in the Church, and their soft staccato singing contrasted strangely with the more refined music of the English voices. In the afternoon the services were for Eskimo only. After worshipping in a snow hut at camp it was a great comfort to come into the Church where everything was clean, where the atmospheric conditions were somewhat more normal, and where no unseemly spectacles disturbed one's thoughts and meditations."

Percy Broughton

The Unknown Missionary

Not much is known of the Arctic missionary Percy Brough-ton. He served the Anglican Church at Lake Harbour for one brief year, and met a tragic end. He is largely forgot-ten today.

Percy Broughton arrived in Lake Harbour (now Kimmirut) on Sunday, September 17, 1911. He had departed by ship from Halifax, accompanied by the grand old man of Arctic missionary work, Reverend Edmund Peck. Two missionaries greeted them at Lake Harbour. Julian Bilby and Archibald Lang Fleming had established the mission station there two years earlier. From the writings of Peck and Bilby we glean only the sparsest of informa-tion about Broughton.

Peck described him as "a devoted young man from Wycliffe

College" and noted while aboard ship that "he is evidently very practical." In teaching him the fundamentals of the Inuktitut language while travelling north, Peck found him to be "very intelligent and soon grasps difficult points." He had met Inuit on the Baffin coast before, while travelling by ship to Hudson Bay, where he had worked in an unknown capacity among the Cree. Bilby noted Broughton's arrival at Lake Harbour tersely but provided no information on him, not even his first name: "I was delighted ... to welcome Mr. Peck and a Mr. Broughton to the station."

The Inuit soon gave the newcomer the name Nagligusuktuq— "the one who cares."

Peck had earlier decided that one of the missionaries at Lake Harbour would leave for furlough on the ship that year, and the other would remain for another year with Broughton. But at the last minute Samuel Sainsbury, a crew member of the ship, volunteered to stay with Broughton and act as assistant missionary. Peck decided on the spot that both Bilby and Fleming would leave with him, and Broughton and Sainsbury would remain at the post. Any orientation that they received from Bilby and Fleming was hurried, as the ship left the following day.

Coincidentally, on that day the Hudson's Bay Company ship *Pelican* arrived to establish that company's first trading station on Baffin Island. It would be staffed by members of the Ford family from the Labrador coast, settlers who spoke Inuktitut.

Percy Broughton's terrible ordeal began in the spring of 1912 while he was on a dog sled journey with Inuit. They had camped for the night. Broughton tells what happened next:

It was a glorious spring morning in March 1912. The sun high in the heavens, shining on the dazzling wilderness, made it almost impossible for me to keep my eyes open. I started for my morning walk while the boys were lashing up the sleighs, leaving my furs, with the exception of a small summer deerskin coat, with the load. There were many tracks one might follow, but I chose that which appeared to be most recent. About noon the track took a sudden turn into the land which did not surprise me, seeing we had travelled about twelve hours over land on the outward journey.

As I trudged along my interest was claimed by the various tracks about me, and my thoughts went rambling on over what might happen if one spent a night out in such an inhospitable country without shelter. Here my day-dreams ended, for suddenly I seemed as one awakened out of sleep, and what is more, realised my position. It was 3 p.m. Perhaps I was miles away from the sleighs, possibly on a wrong track and lost. Perhaps my day-dream would be a reality.[1]

Percy Broughton was indeed miles from the track the Inuit had followed. His dream was about to become a terrible nightmare.

Broughton climbed the highest hill and saw the coast, three miles to the west. It was then that he realized that he had followed the track of a man heading inland to hunt caribou. He knew that he must head for the coast, and if possible get there before dark. But he was tired. Already he had walked seven hours through soft snow. He reached the shore two hours before sunset and began to follow the shoreline.

---

[1] "A Terrible Experience," *Moosonee & Keewatin Mailbag*, Vol. VIII, No. 2, April 1913, 32–33.

In Those Days

Long after dark I walked on until I became so entangled in the hummocks of ice along the shore that I met with obstructions in either direction. Twice I put my foot in the water resting in pools along the shore, so decided I had better stop for the night and get on the land. Every flood tide some water comes up through the cracks in the ice, and remains there until it freezes. Just as I reached the top of the ice and got on the land I fell down between three pieces of rock, which were so embedded as to form an ideal bed. I dug out the snow as best I could with my feet and hands until it was deep enough to shelter me from the wind, and then kept my circulation by bobbing to and fro in a see-saw motion.[2]

He arose at 3:30 and headed for sled tracks on the ice, hoping to fall in with a group of Inuit. About six in the morning he was overcome by "a terrible hunger and craving for food." With nothing else available, he cut a slice from the sleeve of his caribou coat, removed the hair, and ate about six mouthfuls of the skin, which satisfied his craving.

Early that morning the wind changed and blew hard from the northwest. The temperature dropped to minus twenty degrees Fahrenheit, and the ice on which Broughton was travelling broke off and separated from the shore ice. The gap of open water was only about four feet wide, but it extended in both directions as far as he could see.

Under ordinary circumstances one might easily have jumped it, but I failed, being too stiff with the cold, and

---

[2] Ibid., 33.

only went in up to my chest, as I caught the ice the other side. The first thought that struck me was, "I am done for now," but later that beautiful thought "He will carry you through" crowded it out. My hunger and weariness were forgotten; a new life seemed to seize me. Walk? I could walk all day; indeed I must do so to keep from freezing. When I sat down to empty my skin boots and wring out my stockings, the right boot froze so hard that I could not get it on again; my clothes also had been torn, and in this condition I walked the next twenty-five miles.[3]

Most of Broughton's walking was on the sea ice, with occasional detours to land. By early afternoon he reckoned he was about six hours away from an Inuit camp. But his calculation was wrong, and by sunset he was far from safety. Finally he decided to stop for the night.

How can I describe that awful night? Oh, how I looked in vain for a friendly rock to shelter me from the biting wind! How I needed rocks, but found myself on a large open plain! My mittens were frozen too hard to put on, so I used them with my cap for a seat. My coat I took off and put over my knees, but the biting wind pierced through my other clothes as if they were muslin.... My feet were frozen too hard to stand up or walk. Like St. Paul, I wished for the day.

Dawn came at last, and by crawling on my hands and knees I got over the tidal ice and climbed a peak to look for the coast. There, less than half-a-mile in front of me,

---

[3] Ibid.

was the Cape. So, gathering up all the energy I had left, I pressed on, scarcely able to walk ten paces without falling down. But this was a blessing in disguise because it saved my hands from freezing badly. By pulling my coat-sleeve over my hands I was able to finally crawl into the igloos and had just enough vitality left to tell a man to go to the Mission twenty miles away for food and stimulants. Then I became unconscious for about twelve hours.

When I came to I learned that the people had thawed my feet against their bodies and my other frozen parts were thawed in their hands. Seventeen hours after my arrival at the Cape the Eskimo returned with help from the Mission, and the next day the Hudson [sic] Bay Company kindly took me to the station, blind and in great agony. In five days my sight returned, and three weeks later I got my assistant to cut off my toes, while I operated on myself for internal injuries due to the frost.[4]

The medical training that Broughton had received at Wycliffe College stood him in good stead, for he reported, "Five times it was necessary for me to operate on myself."

I've often wondered, in reading missionary biographies, why some missionaries insisted on writing such deprecating opinions about the Inuit with whom they lived and worked. It is all the more remarkable in Percy Broughton's case because he owed his very life to the Inuit. Yet, in writing about his terrible ordeal and his near-death from freezing, he wrote about the Inuit, "Although the Eskimos are so repulsive, they are a loveable people."

---

[4] Ibid., 34.

Broughton was back to work after three weeks, preaching his services from his sickbed. But he was in terrible shape, having frozen his testicles as well as his feet and other body parts. It was May before he could stand up, and he could walk only with a pair of improvised crutches that Sainsbury made for him. He tried to make a trip with Sainsbury to one of the Inuit camps but had to return on the fourth day, too sick to stay longer.

The whaler *Active* arrived on July 24, and he got laudanum and cocaine from the captain. This helped to ease the pain. On August 11 Julian Bilby returned on the Hudson's Bay Company supply ship *Nascopie*. Broughton took passage on that ship, then transferred to the government steamer *Minto*, which carried a doctor, who performed three more operations on the unfortunate missionary on the way south. On November 2, eighty-five days after leaving Lake Harbour, he was transferred to another vessel bound for Canada. He rested in Toronto, where he endured more operations, then left for London, England, and another operation, one that he hoped would be the last.

Unfortunately it didn't turn out well for Broughton. He reached England on December 7 and remained there for a time. Then he returned to Canada in 1913. He next turns up in Auckland, New Zealand, on August 28, arriving there on a steamer, *Makura*, out of Vancouver. A New Zealand newspaper reported that he was en route to Sydney, Australia, where he would meet his fiancée and marry. Ominously, the reporter stated that Broughton was too ill to describe his horrible experiences, but that another passenger who had heard them aboard ship recounted them.

That anonymous person claimed that Broughton told him that the Inuit had deliberately abandoned him on the land. The journalist coloured that part of his article with the observation, "Then the treachery with which the people of the Arctic regions are credited showed itself." But Broughton himself, in his own account of his ordeal, makes no mention of abandonment, instead blaming himself for following the wrong trail.

Broughton did not marry the woman in Australia and returned once more to Canada. After 1913, he disappeared from the pages of missionary publications until a brief mention appeared in July 1916. "Poor Mr. Broughton, I grieve to say, died from the effects of his awful experiences at Lake Harbour," wrote Reverend Peck. A few pages later Peck noted that Broughton died in September 1915 "on account of his terrible injuries."

Percy Broughton died in Port Bickerton, Guysborough County, Nova Scotia, on September 6, 1915, of an overdose of morphine. He was presumably self-medicating because of the continuing pain from his injuries suffered in the Arctic. His tombstone bears the words "His Good Works Follow Him," and "Erected by Friends at Bickerton." He was thirty-one years of age.

Father Turquetil

First Roman Catholic Bishop of the Arctic

Arsène Louis Eugène Turquetil was born July 3, 1876, in Reviers, France. Orphaned at a young age, he was adopted by nuns of a local parish, so it can be truly said that he had a religious upbringing. From a young age, his one desire was to be a missionary. Not just a priest, but a missionary. After completing his studies in France and Belgium, on his ordination to the priesthood in 1899 he was asked his preference for a future ministry; he replied, "Anywhere, as long as it is a mission ... but not in Europe." In fact, his fervent desire was to minister to the Inuit.

He was sent to Canada, where he served the Oblate order for forty-two years. Pope Pius XI once told him, "If I could but visit some missions, yours are the ones I would choose."

His first posting was at Brochet, on Reindeer Lake in northern Saskatchewan. This might seem like an odd place from which to

In Those Days

begin a mission to the Inuit, but in fact it made very good sense. In 1868 Father Alphonse Gasté, the missionary there, had made a visit far to the north to the isolated Ahiarmiut Inuit, who lived at the very edge of the northern forest in the southwest corner of what is now Nunavut.

The Ahiarmiut traded sporadically with the Hudson's Bay Company at Churchill, but Gasté convinced them that it would be more convenient to travel south to Brochet to trade. The missionary knew that at Churchill they were exposed almost exclusively to Protestant ideas. At Brochet he could minister to them directly. The Inuit bought the idea; they continued trading into Brochet until about 1920, by which time independent white traders had taken the trade to them, establishing small posts in the barren lands.

Turquetil made his first trip into Inuit territory in 1901 and continued to minister to the Ahiarmiut who came to Brochet to trade.

In 1910 the Keewatin Vicariate was formed, and Bishop Charlebois chose Turquetil to make plans for a mission within Inuit country. Finally, in 1912, he was sent to establish the Oblate mission at Chesterfield Inlet, which would be his home for so many years. An HBC post had been established there the previous year, and the Oblates knew that Anglican Bibles (though not missionaries) had already reached the area from southern Baffin Island with Inuit who were sometimes transported to the area to work for the whalers.

Still, it took Turquetil many years to make his first conversions. In fact, in 1916 his superiors informed him that the mission would be closed if no conversions could be expected.

But in that year, the miracle happened. Joseph Tuni, a well-known *angakkuq*—a shaman—converted.

Although the priests faced opposition from shamans and had to preach against their influence, calling their methods trickery, they were not above a little deception of their own. Turquetil had received from France a little booklet on the life of Thérèse de Lisieux. (Some years later, she was declared a saint.) The envelope also contained some earth taken from beneath the first coffin of Thérèse, the Little Flower of Lisieux, and a note that it could be used to perform miracles. The next evening, Father Girard surreptitiously approached some Inuit visitors from behind and scattered some of the holy earth on their hair. "The next Sunday, Inuit came to the mass in great numbers," wrote researchers Laugrand and Oosten, "and Tuni announced that he and two other men wished to be baptized with their wives and children."

Some would call this a miracle attributed to Thérèse; others would call it a deception. Father Turquetil, with no apparent sense of irony, wrote: "These poor people take us for sorcerers ... they think we are casting spells and they are afraid, not knowing what spirit we address."

A later priest and commentator, Father Van de Velde, wrote: "In the Eskimo mind, the priest occupies the eminent place formerly held by the sorcerer. Is not the Catholic priest ... a mediator between God and men? Was not the sorcerer also a similar link between the spirits on one side and the Eskimos on the other?" He referenced another missionary who had suggested that the "true translation of the word priest should be 'angakok' [*angakkuq*], that is, sorcerer, and not 'Iksirardjuar' [*iksirarjuaq*] ... which ... means 'the great writer.'"

Advancement followed for Turquetil. He was appointed Prefect Apostolic for Hudson Bay in 1924, Vicar Apostolic in 1931, and consecrated Bishop in 1932. In 1930 he began the construction of St. Theresa's Hospital in Chesterfield Inlet; it was completed two years later.

There was no spirit of ecumenicism in the Arctic at the time. It's been largely forgotten that the Roman Catholics called the Anglicans the "Reds," after the colour of the Anglican prayer book. The Reds were the enemy, not shamanism or superstition. If a follower of the Anglicans wished to convert to Catholicism, he had to turn over his red prayer book to the priest, who was then required to keep it or burn it.

When the Oblates produced the first Catholic hymnal and prayer book in Inuktitut Syllabics, the script bore a decidedly different look than that of the Anglican Syllabics. That is because Turquetil used the Syllabic lettering that he had been familiar with at Brochet, that used for the Chipewyan. It had a much more square and boxy appearance than the Anglican symbols and was quite distinctive.

Catholicism in the Arctic expanded rapidly once established at Chesterfield Inlet. Missions were opened at Eskimo Point (now Arviat, 1924), Southampton Island (1926), Baker Lake (1927), Pond Inlet (1929), Igloolik (1932), Repulse Bay (now Naujaat, 1933), and Pelly Bay (now Kugaaruk, 1935).

When Father Turquetil retired in 1942, he left over thirty missionaries working in the Arctic. He died in 1955 in Washington, D.C. His rule of conduct during this long life and ministry was this: "Know well what you wish to do: do it with all your heart and, no matter what happens, never get discouraged."

Missionary Names in Cumberland Sound

T he first missionary to spend a winter in Baffin Island was Brother Mathias Warmow of the Moravian Church in Greenland. He spent the winter of 1857–58 with the whaling captain William Penny aboard his ship, *Lady Franklin*, near Kekerten in Cumberland Sound.

Unlike most of the white missionaries who would come to Baffin Island decades later, Warmow arrived with a distinct advantage. He could already speak an Inuit dialect, West Greenlandic. Writing about the first Inuit that he met, he noted, "As they understood me, and I them, very well, we were able to converse with but little difficulty." Many of the Inuit in Cumberland Sound understood a little English, having learned it from their interaction with Scottish and American whalers. From the whalers they had learned that a "minister" was coming to instruct them. And so, instead of giving him a descriptive Inuktitut name, as they did with many newcomers, the Inuit simply called him "minister." This displeased Warmow, who noted that he would have preferred they call him by his Christian name, or its Greenlandic equivalent, Matiuse.

It would be three and a half decades before Edmund Peck arrived at Blacklead Island to build his mission there. He arrived with the same advantage that Warmow had had; he already spoke Inuktitut, having learned the language during eight years on the Hudson Bay coast of Quebec. The Inuit gave him a name—Uqammak. It means "the one who speaks well" and is derived from the verb root *uqaq-*, which signifies speaking. Stories of Uqammak have been passed down through the generations, and the name is still remembered today.

In 1894 Peck brought with him a twenty-two-year-old layman, Joseph Parker. As preparation for his missionary work, Parker had taken a few months of medical training. To travel to the mission station, he signed on as doctor of the whaling ship *Alert*. At the mission station he threw himself into the task of learning Inuktitut and made rapid progress. He ministered to the sick, and the Inuit gave him a name, Luktaakuluk—"the little doctor" or "the dear doctor." Inuit words don't start with *d*, and *luktaaq* was the closest they could come to pronouncing "doctor." The suffix *-kuluk* is one signifying endearment or smallness. Unfortunately the little doctor drowned in a boating accident two years later.

That same year another missionary arrived at Blacklead. He was Charles Sampson, and he remained with the mission until 1900, when he returned to England and resigned. He subsequently returned as a trader. I know of no Inuktitut name for him. They may have simply called him *ajuriqsuiji*, perhaps with a descriptive suffix added. *Ajuriqsuiji* is the general term for a Protestant minister and can roughly be translated as "the teacher" or "the instructor."

When Julian Bilby arrived from England to join Peck and Sampson, he endeared himself to the Inuit through his devotion to language study and his interest in the local way of life and customs. He was rewarded with the Inuktitut name Ilataaq. The first part of this name, *ila*, is a noun meaning "relative" or "friend"; *-taaq* is a suffix showing acquisition. Perhaps his name should best be translated as "our new friend."

E. W. T. Greenshield arrived to join Peck in 1901, the summer that Bilby left for furlough in England. He too immersed himself in language study and was popular among the Inuit. They graced him with a name that simply added an additional suffix to Bilby's name, calling him Ilataaqauk—"another new friend."

That completes the roster of white missionaries to Cumberland Sound prior to the movement of the mission station from Blacklead Island to Pangnirtung in the 1920s.

Rules of Life and Death

Among the inland Paallirmiut—the people who lived around the great lake Hikuligjuaq and the upper reaches of the Kazan River—whom Knud Rasmussen visited in 1922, many customs differed considerably from those of the coast dwellers he had previously met.

Rasmussen felt that their religion was a "pronouncedly inland religion." He was fascinated to learn that the complex taboo rules that the coast dwellers—the Aivilingmiut—were required to follow were much more lax among the inlanders. He felt that they lived under "natural conditions that traditionally were indigenous and natural to them."

He was particularly interested in the differences in customs surrounding death.

He recorded these customs as follows:

When a person dies, the body must only remain in the house overnight, it being sufficient the first night to wrap the shroud round it, tie it up in the burial skin and lay it right up at the back of the platform. Five days after a death all the people in the village must do a sort of penance, refraining from eating entrails, head, marrow and similar food that is forbidden to the unclean. Nor may meat be taken from the caches during these five days ... only freshly caught animals may be brought home. Hunting in these five days is not forbidden and salmon may be fished in the lakes. But a caribou must never be flensed in the house where a corpse has lain....

When the corpse is to be taken out of the house or tent, it is always, as among the coast dwellers, passed through the rear wall, never through the doorway. For if a corpse is taken out through the doorway, all the game will become shy and disappear and the people of the village will starve to death.

The dead, who ... is tied up in a caribou skin, is carried on another caribou skin to the place where he or she is to be buried. This is done by the relatives, both men and women....

In the five days during which the relatives mourn a dead person and do penance, the grave must be visited morning and evening, and there the loud lamentations are voiced. They say, "We call; to the dead to make him return again, though we know he cannot hear."

It seems to be general that the period for doing penance after a death is always five days, whether it is for a man or a woman. The custom of the coast dwellers that in these five days the women must wear their hair loose, is not known.

Those who have helped with a dead body need not throw their clothing away; it is sufficient to cut off a narrow edging of the sleeve band and at the same time discard their caribou-skin mittens....

As soon as the five days are over, sparks are struck with a fire-stone on the floor by a man who has especially effective amulets.... No one is afraid to mention the name of the departed, and if, for instance, a visitor comes, they say quite openly that he or she is dead. The custom of setting a sledge up on end before a house where there has been a death is not known, nor do they lay either knives or ulos [women's knives] under their pillow.

Offerings after a death are rarely made. Yet I have seen some men who have lost a wife to whom they were very much attached, bring garments and sleeping skins to the grave.[1]

One striking difference between the customs of the coastal Aivilingmiut and the inland Inuit was in the treatment of widows immediately upon their bereavement. Rasmussen noted, "Widows among many coast dwellers must subject themselves to extremely severe and difficult taboos until a whole year has elapsed after the death. Among the inland dwellers a widow may eat with others after five days."

The number five seems to have been of great significance to the Paallirmiut, for it also played a role in the taboo behaviour

---

[1] Knud Rasmussen, *Intellectual Culture of the Caribou Eskimos. Report of the Fifth Thule Expedition 1921-24*, Vol. VII, No. 2 (Copenhagen: Gyldendalske Boghandel, 1930), 62–64.

that applied to the family of a man who had died: "Among the coast dwellers, it will also be remembered, for a whole year after a man's death none of his housemates had to do any work with the knife. Everything they needed making must be made by others. This is only in force for five days here."

Rasmussen also spent considerable time among a different group of Inuit, the Qaernermiut of the Baker Lake area, and wrote extensively about their beliefs as well.

Their "Rules of Life," as Rasmussen described them, amounted to an oppressive set of taboos that regulated all aspects of their lives. Here are some examples:

Dogs must never gnaw at a caribou antler. If they do, they deprive the owner of his quarry.

No one, except women with special amulets, may sew or cut bearded seal skin bought from the coast dwellers.

A young woman with an infant, while on a sledge journey, must never eat anything while passing a lake.

A young woman with an infant may not eat salmon heads or salmon cooked with the head, or salmon on the whole if the entrails have not been removed immediately after the fish was caught. The same applies to naturally dead salmon or the meat of a caribou that has been shot in the heart.

No one may eat salmon on the same day that berries have been eaten.

Men must not eat milt [the male reproductive glands of fish]. If they do, they are deprived of their sexual impulse.

Men must not eat the eyes of animals, salmon, etc. as this gives bad eyesight.

In Those Days

When a milk tooth falls out, it must be placed under the platform skin [the caribou skin of the sleeping platform], the owner desiring a tooth of the great head that once was this caribou's head. The following magic verse is then sung:

"Great head, take my tooth to be your tooth
And give me your tooth to be my tooth
That I may have a tooth that often eats rich fat
That often eats tongue
A fine tooth
A hard tooth, that will not break."

Women may not eat with people whom they have never seen before.

Women may never eat with men.

Women with children may not eat salmon that have not been gutted immediately after being killed.

If a trout that is called *heeq* is caught in a salmon net, it should be thrown alive into the water again, or no salmon will be caught.

If a loon gets into the salmon net, it should be allowed to fly away. If not, no more salmon will be caught. If the loon has died in the net, one should take care to place it where the dogs cannot eat it.[2]

---

[2] Ibid., 64–65.

"Coming Up Jesusy"

At the Blacklead Mission, in its heyday, religious instruction was easily obtained. But most Inuit did not live at or near a mission. For them, Peck sent Bibles and prayer books with Inuit who came to trade at Blacklead. This literature was passed along from one Inuit camp to the next. Peck also arranged to send his books north to Pond Inlet on Joseph Bernier's expeditions and on traders' vessels. The books he sent were written in the Inuktitut Syllabic orthography. Literacy was quickly obtained using this system, so one Inuk could teach another. Very soon, Inuit who had never seen a missionary—indeed, never seen any white man—were literate and able to read Peck's material.

Understanding, however, was a different matter. The trader Wilfred Caron's Inuit wife, Panikpak, told her granddaughter that she

In Those Days

and her family got their first Bibles from Nakungajuq—Captain Murray, who commanded Captain Munn's trading ship, the *Albert*. Some of the Inuit didn't know what they were for, so they took them apart and used the pages as wallpaper for their dwellings.

To understand why Inuit converted so readily to Christianity, it is necessary to understand something of Inuit traditional beliefs.

Traditional religion relied on belief in a number of spirits, adhering to numerous taboos to regulate behaviour, and following the injunctions of *angakkuit*—shamans—to placate the spirits offended through violation of the taboos. Taboos were legion; they had become pervasive and unduly restrictive. Indeed, they had become so numerous that living a normal life was hampered by them.

The first missionaries did not arrive in northern Baffin Island until 1929, but in the years before that, Inuit had developed their own conversion ritual, a rite of passage known as *siqqitirniq*. It was a way of integrating selected features of Christianity into the Inuit religious system, and a way for the Inuit to free themselves from certain ritual injunctions, replacing them with less onerous proscriptions on their behaviour.

Although all Inuit in the Canadian Arctic eventually embraced Christianity, many before the actual arrival of missionaries, the peculiar practices of siqqitirniq were limited to Inuit of northern Baffin Island, the Iglulik area, and the northern Kivalliq coast.

In 1999, an elder from Pond Inlet recalled his people's conversion to Christianity, the process of going through siqqitirniq, almost a century earlier:

> They cut the seal open and took out the intestines, the liver, the heart, the eyes, and the tongue and cut them into small

pieces…. People lined up and were given a piece of meat to put into their mouth. People were asked why they wanted to go through this ceremony. Everyone of them replied, '… because we want to become Christian.'… Everyone of us was given a piece of meat. We did this because all those parts of the seal, the heart, and the intestine were all parts of the *pittailiniq*, the taboos. They were no longer to be observed. There wouldn't be any part of the seal that people would have to abstain from eating. This was not just the case for seal, but for all other animals as well. There was not going to be any more abstaining from eating any part of the animal.[1]

This aspect of siqqitirniq, the purposeful consumption of certain foods, was, then, a blatant flouting of the old taboos, a visible act of rebellion and a sign that the person was following a new belief that contradicted and replaced those taboos.

The elder's description of the new ritual continues:

After this happened, whenever anyone would arrive from elsewhere, we would all go down and shake hands…. It became a new ritual. People who accepted religion shook hands. They started to pray. What they wanted to do was rid themselves of all that was from the past, whether it be the *angakkuit* or other ways of living. They were all brought together into the largest *iglu*…. They would come together and get rid of the

---

[1] Rachel Uyarasuk, quoted in Victor Tungilik and Rachel Uyarasuk, (Frédéric Laugrand and Jarich Oosten, eds.), *The Transition to Christianity* (Iqaluit: Nunavut Arctic College, 1999), 123–24.

wrong-doings they had done, by confessing them.

When [people] started following religion, the angakkuit let go of their powers, and people let go of their *pittailiniq*.[2]

The phenomenon of siqqitirniq developed in the Pond Inlet area under the very noses of the rival traders operating there. Although largely unremarked by the traders, Inuit culture was undergoing a transition, a change that would free it from the taboos of traditional religion but bind the people, nonetheless, to a new set of beliefs, sometimes equally unreasonable but easier to follow.

The late Noah Piugaattuk, an elder in Igloolik, noted in 1991 that "the older people made it known that they found it so much easier to live with the new religion in comparison to the taboo beliefs that they had to live with prior to that time."

Piugaattuk remembered that Christianity was introduced to his area not by missionaries, but by other Inuit who had learned of it from missionaries. Those Inuit, intermediaries really in the transmission of the new religion, had an imperfect understanding of the Bible. Indeed, some may not even have possessed a Bible at all. So Piugaattuk remarked, "It took some time for us to learn about Christianity. It was very difficult to grasp the teaching of Christianity at first. The absence of the bible made it even harder."

With the practice of siqqitirniq came confession. Confession had always been a part of shamanistic ritual; one had had to confess one's transgressions of the taboos that regulated behaviour, for it was those transgressions that were responsible for adversity and hardship. Now the old emphasis on confession was simply

---

[2] Ibid., 124.

grafted onto the new observance of Christianity.

One of the traders active in the Pond Inlet area, Captain Henry Toke Munn of the Arctic Gold Exploration Syndicate, wrote that, at a meeting in a snow house, a native man stood up before the owner and confessed, "Three years ago, when you were away, I stole your wife." The other man replied, after a lengthy pause, "That is all right now," and let the matter drop.

Munn made the observation that people generally confessed to transgressions that had happened some time ago; recent sins were never confessed.

* * *

It is likely that the active brand of religion that resulted in the almost wholesale conversion of the Pond Inlet Inuit from their adherence to shamanism to a faith in Christianity was brought to northern Baffin Island by a man named Akumalik. From Tununiq—the Pond Inlet area—he had travelled to Cumberland Sound, where he had encountered Christianity at the Blacklead mission. But by the time of his journey, the last Qallunaaq missionary had been gone from there for some years, and the mission was maintained by Inuit lay catechists who had no formal training in religion. The missionaries Peck, Bilby, and Greenshield had trained them well, but still, to some extent they were on their own to interpret the words of the Bible in their own way. We will never know exactly what Akumalik learned of Christianity while there. But when he returned to Pond Inlet in the late 1910s, it was with Bibles and some knowledge of their contents.

Back home, Akumalik actively proselytized and made many converts. He travelled extensively by dog sled, bringing his message of Christianity to scattered hunting camps. People still remember one of his eccentricities: when he wanted to pray in public with the people, he would stand facing them, then look down at the ground and move around in a circle the way a dog does when preparing to lie down.

Some of what we know about Akumalik comes from the pen of the fur trader Captain Munn. His company was active in northern Baffin Island, and Munn himself spent time there. He knew Akumalik well. Akumalik's wife, Arnaujaq, was the sister of Tom Kunuk, Munn's main native employee, well known by his Inuktitut name, Takijualuk.

Munn thought that Akumalik was very intelligent and described him in his condescending way as "an excellent native." But he thought that his explanations of Christian tenets were vague and crude, and only enabled his followers to tack the new belief on to their older one. He noted that those among Akumalik's followers who were able to talk the English jargon that Inuit used to communicate with traders used the odd expression "coming up Jesusy" to describe their embracing of the new faith.

Munn's comments on many aspects of Inuit life would today be dubbed as racist. He felt that the Inuk was "a hunter by task and heredity." "Unspoilt," he wrote, "the Eskimo is a likeable, happy, somewhat irresponsible child in his dealing with white men."

Predictably, Munn didn't like the advent of Christianity. "I frankly prefer ... the unconverted native Eskimo," he wrote, adding, "and I think his own animistic 'religion' fulfils best his simple needs in that respect." Munn wrote that his associate, William Duval, who had spent half a century among the Inuit, "considers the unconverted native to be more truthful, self-reliant, honest and kinder to his old people and children. He has found the unconverted native always more generous in sharing his food in times of hunger."

During the winter of 1921, Tom Kunuk often asked Munn to explain the "Tree-ni-tee." Munn was perhaps not the best choice for religious instructor, but he nonetheless made an attempt at answering Tom's questions. That winter a young widow who had recently converted to Christianity became pregnant. She insisted that she had had nothing to do with a man since her conversion; inspired by stories of the virgin birth, she claimed that her child-to-be was a "Jesusy baby."

What developed was a crude form of Christianity, manifested, in the words of one author, in "singing hymns and reading bibles, in shaking hands and waving white flags." It has been described as a "weird blend of Anglicanism and Inuit spirituality."

* * *

Two men in the Pond Inlet area became particularly enthralled by this new religion, modified it to suit their own purposes, and exported it to the Igulik area. They were the father-and-son team of Umik and Nuqallaq.

Umik had originally come from the Iglulik area but had lived in Tununiq for some years. Noah Piugaattuk recalled late in life, "When he [Umik] understood something about the Christian religion, he started to teach others about the new religion and moved to this area [Iglulik] once again to convert others to Christianity."

The move to Iglulik took place in May 1921. Nuqallaq travelled with his father. He had recently killed the trader Robert Janes, for which he would eventually stand trial for murder. But he wasn't running away. Indeed, he had gone to Captain Munn, who had already reported the killing to the police in Ottawa, to ask if he objected to him leaving. Munn gave his permission, feeling that he would be easily found if needed.

Umik, the father, became the main proponent of Christianity in the Iglulik area. One elder in Arctic Bay told me in 1980 how Umik had baptized him in his youth, giving him the name Ikuallariktuq—the one that burns with a bright flame.

History would have recorded very little first-hand information about the new religion's arrival in Iglulik had it not been for the presence of the scientists and explorers of the Danish Fifth Thule Expedition in Foxe Basin in the winter of 1921–22. When the archaeologist Therkel Mathiassen and his party arrived at a southerly camp of the Iglulik Inuit that winter, he noted, "We saw a white rag on a pole outside the snow house and, when we arrived at the place we were surprised by the inhabitants shaking hands with us; even the tiniest child had to do it." Mathiassen found a crucifix carved from ivory hanging inside a snow house, perhaps an influence from the Roman Catholic mission that had been established to the south at Chesterfield Inlet in 1912. When he attempted to buy it, he was told that it was a powerful amulet. At other camps they observed the same kind of white flag and experienced the same hand-shaking, signs that the people were part of Umik's flock.

Mathiassen also noted that "his religion included abstention from work on Sundays, gathering now and then in his snow house and singing hymns which he had taught them, and, what is more, the hunters were to bring their booty to him and he would distribute it." Nuqallaq acted as his assistant priest and "did not lift a finger in hunting either." When people arrived at a settlement or left, everyone gathered to sing a hymn and there was hand-shaking all round. Mathiassen commented that "even the dogs' paws were taken."

At Iglulik, Mathiassen met the prophet himself, whom he described as "an elderly, intelligent man." Although Umik had only been back from Tununiq since May, the whole Iglulik area had been won over to his religion "in a flash," even though some of the older people objected to it. One, Tagurnaaq, scornfully remarked that "Aapaq has become a Christian for her food." By this she meant that Aapaq, a young woman who had recently given birth and would therefore have been under a number of food prohibitions, had conveniently avoided them by converting to Christianity.

Mathiassen thought that Umik "ruled there [Iglulik] absolutely." He was a liberal man who permitted polygamy and offered to lend his wife to Mathiassen's party for their stay. Mathiassen declined the offer. Umik himself was in the habit of exchanging wives for a year at a time with another man.

By the spring of 1922, Umik's brand of religion reached Repulse Bay (now Naujaat), and many converted despite the presence of a Catholic mission there.

Peter Freuchen, another member of the Danish expedition, met Umik and Nuqallaq near Iglulik in May of 1922. He remarked that the two had come down from the Pond Inlet area the previous spring and "commenced to practise some supposed Cristian [sic] religion, and converted everybody at Igloolick [sic], which made them both rather big men amongst the natives of the settlement." They had both stopped hunting, but all the game killed by the natives was brought to them, to be divided as they wished. In a book he wrote some years later, Freuchen described Nuqallaq as being his father's "assistant and truant officer."

Freuchen said that Nuqallaq "worked a racket of constituting himself a 'customs department,' and anyone who came to

In Those Days

Igdloolik *[sic]* to trade had to hand over half his goods to Nuqallaq." Freuchen wrote that Umik and Nuqallaq forbade the practice of wife exchange except for themselves; they, "being superior beings, would be able to borrow anyone's wife they wanted—and their wants were insatiable."

Freuchen also thought that Nuqallaq was cruel. He wrote, "Nuqallaq was the only Eskimo I ever laid hands on. He had a very pleasant little wife whom he foully mistreated ... I saw Nuqallaq swing his wife round by the hair and kick her in the belly ... and I took him between my fingers and roughed him up a bit. He bellowed with rage and yelled that he had killed one white man and could easily kill another. So I had to rough him a bit more and throw him through the wall of the house."

Finley McInnes, an officer with the Royal Canadian Mounted Police, visited Iglulik in the spring of 1923 and noted, "They are very enthusiastic over religion, which they follow in their own crude style, singing hymns and reading from their Testament several times a day. The most attractive pastime, however, is trying to count the number of the pages and the hymns."

He observed that those who had been Christianized demonstrated this by carrying a white flag attached to the sled while travelling. When a visitor was seen to approach a settlement, the entire adult population would line up side by side in a prominent place in front of the snow houses and begin to sing a hymn when the visitor was within hearing distance. The new arrival was expected to stop his team and stand beside his sled until the hymn was finished, at which time each singer would greet him with three shakes of the hand. These same formalities were followed when a village resident returned after only a few hours' absence.

Therkel Mathiassen suggested that "if no reinforcements in the form of missionaries arrive for this new 'religion,' if this collection of half digested or undigested maxims can be called a religion, it will presumably disappear just as quickly as it came when it no longer has the interest of novelty."

Roman Catholic and Anglican missionaries did not arrive in Pond Inlet until 1929, and each built permanent missions there. It was not until 1932 that Catholics established the first mission in the Iglulik area.

The Spread of
Syllabics

The Syllabic writing system used by many Canadian Inuit was created by a Wesleyan missionary for use among the Cree Indians of Manitoba in the 1840s. In the 1850s two Church Missionary Society missionaries, Horden and Watkins, adapted that system for use with Inuktitut—the language of the Inuit. But both of those missionaries worked in the extreme southern reaches of Inuit territory, and the system did not spread until Reverend Edmund James Peck arrived in Little Whale River and began to work almost exclusively with Inuit. He learned Inuktitut, translated material into Syllabics, sent his translations off to England, and succeeded in having a body of religious literature made available for Inuit.

Peck spent the years from 1876 to 1892 on the Hudson Bay

coast of Quebec, at Little Whale River and Fort George, with only one year off for a holiday back in England. In 1894 he relocated to Blacklead Island in Cumberland Sound and spent four periods of two years each there, leaving permanently in 1905.

Each of the books produced by Peck had a "Syllabarium" at the beginning—a Syllabic chart. The chart was organized in four columns, one for each of the vowel sounds. (Purists, at this point, may wish to remind me that the vowel in the first column was really a digraph.) Down the left side there was sometimes a list of English consonants, which represented the first letter of each syllable except those in the top row. The symbols in the four columns (again, excluding the top row) each represented a combination of an initial consonant and the corresponding vowel. Each of the symbols in the top row represented a vowel with no consonant. And down the right side was a row of characters called "finals."

The books Peck gave the Inuit were passed hand to hand up and down the coast, from camp to camp. The Syllabic system for Inuit was so simple that each Inuk who learned it became a teacher for the next person.

People taught each other the system by rote, the book in front of them, pointing to the symbols and reciting *ai, i, u, a, pai, pi, pu, pa, tai, ti, tu, ta.* And so on. Monotonous? Probably. Effective? Definitely.

And so the system spread far beyond the areas that had been reached by missionaries.

In 1922, in the Kivalliq interior, Knud Rasmussen listened to a song contest between two men, deriding each other in verse for their shortcomings. One man, Utahania, having been excoriated by Kanaihuaq for his transgressions, responded in kind to his tormentor, who, he sang, was guilty of having learned "the sign alphabet of the missionaries" and had become snobbish as a result. Rasmussen's text provides the song in his transcription of Inuktitut, and then in the following English translation:

Ivmaiya - ayai
Is there any sort of reason
Aya,
Why the Lord of the White Men
Should pay heed to your words?
Ivmaiya,
Is he to put any trust in your words
Because you and you Tupialaaq
Drove him up to those
Who dwell to the east of us?
And yet all the same he listened to you
(and thought you were wise)
Because you could write down speaking signs
With "writing hand",
And make your speech
Like that of a chieftain.
And now I sing
Just to be nasty,
A song such as that a bird sings
With its beak
Here in the qaggje.[1]

---

[1] Knud Rasmussen, *Intellectual Culture of the Caribou Eskimos: Report of the Fifth Thule Expedition 1921-24*. Vol. VII, No. 2 (Copenhagen: Gyldendalske Boghandel, 1930), 78.

(A *qaggiq*, here spelled *qaggje*, is a large communal snow house.)

In 1990, Inuit participating in the Igloolik Oral History Project, talked about Iqipiriaq, who had lived at Avvajja, and his struggle with Syllabics:

> He knew nothing about white people and the language. He knew nothing about letters or anything like that, as a matter of fact he made a song about it. He had tried in vain to learn letters but he could not learn them so he made a song about them instead. It goes something like this:

> This letter that looks like a hook,
> I wish I could learn what it is,
> Gai Gii Guu Ga, Gai Gii Guu Ga.[2]

A year later, the aged Noah Piugaattuk also remembered Iqipiriaq's difficulty and his famous little song: "I remember the time when some of the people knew how to write while some did not. Iqipiriaq was one of those that never did get to learn the symbols of the writing system. He tried hard to learn but he never caught on. As a matter of fact he composed a song about the symbols of the writing system, hoping he could remember the symbols."

Most Inuit in the eastern Arctic did learn Syllabics, many well before they ever saw a missionary. This is a tribute to the ease of the system developed by Horden and Watkins and revised by Peck, a system that spread largely through the "each one teach one" approach.

---

[2] Interview with Pauli Kunnuk, interviewed by Louis Tapardjuk, 23 January 1990, Tape #IE-087, Igloolik Oral History Project.

Orpingalik

"All My Being Is Song"

In 1923 Knud Rasmussen and two Greenlandic travelling companions, Qaavigarsuaq and Arnarulunnguaq, travelled by dog sled from Hudson Bay into Nattilik country, what is now the northern Kivalliq and eastern Kitikmeot regions. For the first part of their journey they were accompanied by two Kivalliq Inuit, Taparti and Anarqaaq.

The first Nattilingmiut they encountered were a father and son, Orpingalik and Kanajoq, who were on their way to Repulse Bay (now Naujaat) to trade. It was a fortuitous meeting, for Orpingalik was a shaman held in high regard by his people. Rasmussen thought him an "interesting man, well at home in the old traditions of his tribe" and possessed of a "fertile wit." He was an impressive hunter, a strong archer, and the quickest kayak-man of all in pursuing caribou herds crossing rivers and lakes.

But above all, Orpingalik was a poet. The explorer described his sensitive mind as "luxuriant" and remarked that he was always singing when he had nothing else to do. Orpingalik described his songs as his breath, so necessary to him that they were part and parcel of himself. He told Rasmussen that his songs, which were of his own composition, were "comrades in solitude."

Rasmussen asked Orpingalik how many songs he had composed, and the hunter-poet responded, "How many songs I have I cannot tell you. I keep no count of such things. There are so many occasions in one's life when a joy or a sorrow is felt in such a way that the desire comes to sing; and so I only know that I have many songs. All my being is song, and I sing as I draw breath."

Orpingalik shared with Rasmussen a song that the poet himself called "My Breath," a song he wrote during a period of despondency as a result of a long illness:

I will sing a song,
A little song of myself.
Sick I have lain since autumn
And have turned weak as a child.
Unaya, Unaya.

Sorrowful, I would that
My wife were gone to another house
To a man who could be her refuge,
Secure and firm as the thick winter ice.
Sorrowful, I would she were gone

In Those Days

To a better protector,
Now that I have no strength myself
To rise from my bed.
Unaya, Unaya.

Do you know your fate?
So little you know of yourself.
Now I lie faint and cannot rise,
And only my memories are strong.
Unaya. Unaya.

Beasts of the hunt! Big game!
Oft the fleeing quarry I chased!
Let me live it again and remember,
Forgetting my weakness.
Unaya. Unaya.

Let me recall the great white polar bear,
High up its back body,
Snout in the snow, it came!
He really believed
He alone was a male
And ran towards me.
Unaya. Unaya.

It threw me down again and again,
Then breathless departed and lay down to rest,
Hid by a mound on a floe. Heedless it was, and unknowing
That I was to be its fate.
Deluding itself that he alone was a male,

And unthinking, that I too was a man!
Unaya. Unaya.

I shall never forget that great blubber-beast, a fjord seal
I killed from the sea ice early, long before dawn,
While my companions at home still lay like the dead,
Faint from failure and hunger, sleeping.
With meat and with swelling blubber I returned so quickly
As if merely running over ice to view a breathing hole there.
And yet it was an old and cunning male seal.
But before he had even breathed
My harpoon head was fast, mortally deep in his neck.

That was the manner of me then.
Now I lie feeble on my bench
Unable even to get a little blubber
For my wife's stone lamp.
The time, the time will not pass,
While dawn gives place to dawn
And spring is upon the village.
Unaya. Unaya.

How long shall I lie here?
How long?
And how long must she go a-begging
For fat for her lamp,
For skins for clothing
And meat for a meal?
A helpless thing—a defenceless woman.
Unaya. Unaya.

In Those Days

Do you know yourself?
So little you know of yourself!
While dawn gives place to dawn,
And spring is upon the village.
Unaya. Unaya.[1]

---

[1] Knud Rasmussen, *The Netsilik Eskimos: Social Life and Spiritual Culture. Report of the Fifth Thule Expedition 1921–24*, Vol. VIII, No.1–2 (Copenhagen: Gyldendalske Boghandel, 1931), 321–23, with some adaptations from p. 15.

The Power of
Magic Words

In 1922, the year before Knud Rasmussen met the Nattilik poet and hunter Orpingalik, the hunter had suffered a tragedy and lost one of his sons, Inugjaq.

On a journey in the interior, Orpingalik and his youngest son were ferrying their belongings over a wide and swift-running river on an ice pan. The current was strong and suddenly caught the pan, and one side was forced down so deep into the river that it turned over. Both father and son were immediately at the mercy of the river, which carried them downstream.

Orpingalik was knocked unconscious against a rock. When he came to, he was lying half in the water and half on the riverbank, his head being knocked against a stone by the regular wash of the waves. The pain quickly brought him to his senses, and a quick glance at the sun told him that he had been uncon-scious for some time. Suddenly, he realized his circumstances and began to look frantically for his son. He found Inugjaq far-ther down the river.

Rasmussen continues the story:

> He carried him up to the bank and tried to call him to life with a magic song. It was not long before a caterpillar crawled up on the face of the corpse and began to go round its mouth, round and round. Not long afterwards the son began to breathe very faintly, and then other small creatures of the earth crawled on to his face, and this was a sign that he would come to life again.
>
> But in his joy Orpingalik went home to his tent and brought his wife to help him, taking with him a sleeping skin to lay their son on while working to revive him. But hardly had the skin touched the son when he ceased breath-ing, and it was impossible to put life into him again. Later on it turned out that the reason why the magic words had lost their power was that in the sleeping skin there was a patch that had once been touched by a menstruating woman, and her uncleanness had made the magic words powerless and killed the son.[1]

Another powerful Nattilingmiut man, Qaqortingneq, later offered Rasmussen some insight into Orpingalik's tragedy:

---

[1] Knud Rasmussen, *The Netsilik Eskimos: Social Life and Spiritual Culture. Report of the Fifth Thule Expedition 1921-24.* Vol. VIII, No.1–2 (Copenhagen: Gylden-dalske Boghandel, 1931), 321–23, with some adaptations from pp. 11–12.

"People say that the ice floe on which Orpingalik was crossing the river was so large that it ought not to have capsized in the current. But they say that it was as if the floe suddenly met with some resistance that forced it down under the waters of the river. Therefore it is believed that the cause of the disaster was magic words, bad magic words that rebounded upon their own master: irinaliut utirtuq inungminut."

Qaqortingneq offered Rasmussen an explanation of what he assumed to be the cause of the ill fortune that befell Orpingalik and his son. Uncharacteristically, it involved a white man, but this is perhaps indicative of the rapid culture change that was beginning to occur in that isolated part of the Arctic.

During the previous year, Captain Jean Berthe, a trader with the Hudson's Bay Company, had made a trip to Pelly Bay (now Kugaaruk) to trade. Inugjaq was blamed for tampering with one of the trader's observation instruments that lay on his sled, and the trader scolded the young man.

Orpingalik felt offended by this but said nothing to the trader. Instead he composed some evil magic words intended to kill Berthe before the end of the year. But the words had not been powerful enough to do the job.

Qaqortingneq explained that "a formula of wicked words like that must kill if there is any power in it; and if it does not kill the one it is made for, it turns against its creator, and if it cannot kill him either, one of his nearest must pay with his life."

The Inuit believed, quite simply, that Captain Berthe was a greater shaman than Orpingalik, and that the magic words had no choice but to turn against their source. But Orpingalik was also a shaman of some repute; when the evil words were unable to kill him either, they turned against and killed his son.

In Those Days

Captain Berthe was apparently a popular man among the Inuit. He was unaware of any of this. He had scolded the young man and that, as far as he knew, was the end of it.

Rasmussen, always analytical, found this whole episode to be illustrative of two characteristics of Inuit: the habit of concealing anger while contemplating revenge, and the exaggerated family feeling of *sirnaaniq*, which ensures that an Inuk will always side with his family. Rasmussen observed simply and in conclusion, "They do not tolerate having their children corrected by others."

Mercy Flight to Arctic Bay

A medical evacuation flight—or medivac, in Northern jargon—is nothing out of the ordinary in the modern Arctic. They happen routinely, a number of them every week, adding to the skyrocketing costs of medical services in the North.

But in 1938, medivacs were unheard of. Inuit lived and died in remote camps, largely unknown to officialdom, untended by doctors or nurses. The resident doctors in Pangnirtung and Chesterfield Inlet in the 1930s were anomalies, and their reach did not extend much beyond their immediate areas. Traders, police, and missionaries in the isolated posts that dotted the map of the Arctic took their chances when they accepted their assignments. Some had a minimum of medical training and were able to attend to the minor ailments of both their white colleagues and Inuit in proximity to their posts. But if local resources failed, death usually awaited.

In 1938 a Roman Catholic priest, Father Julien Cochard, lay seriously ill in his mission tent at Arctic Bay, the most northerly Catholic mission in the world. The Hudson's Bay Company post stood a short distance away, and its manager, Allen Scott, discovered the perilous condition of the priest. He sent a radio message to Bishop Clabaut, who was aboard the *Nascopie* at Churchill. It read: "Father Julien Cochard very ill for nine days. Temperature 105 degrees. Severe pains in left side. Takes no nourishment. Please help."

There was no possibility of rescue by ship. But another opportunity was immediately at hand. Father Paul Schulte, the Flying Priest, was based at Churchill with a small amphibious plane. Schulte had honed his skills as a pilot with the German Air Force during the First World War. Following the war, he became an Oblate priest. After his best friend—they had both been ordained on the same day—died in Africa without medical attention, Schulte founded and incorporated the Missionary International Vehicular Association, dedicated to providing automobiles, boats, and airplanes for the service of missions throughout the world.

At Churchill, Schulte had a small plane, a Stinson Reliant, on floats. Named the *St. Luke*, it was nicknamed the *Flying Cross*. On August 9, when Schulte received the message about Father Cochard's illness, he immediately offered to fly to Arctic Bay to rescue the ailing priest. But his bishop reminded him that there was no gasoline to refuel his plane at Arctic Bay. Fortunately, the previous year, Schulte had sent six barrels of gas and one barrel of oil by ship to Igloolik. He would refuel there.

His mechanic, Brother Beaudoin, worked that night to get the plane ready for what would be a 2,200-mile return journey. Pilot and mechanic took off early in the morning and landed in heavy rain at eight thirty a.m. in Chesterfield Inlet, the first stop on their journey. By two in the afternoon they were in Repulse Bay (now Naujaat), where they again refuelled. They reached Igloolik at six thirty in the evening. With his tanks full and twenty-four-hour daylight in his favour, Schulte left Igloolik at nine p.m. He needed optimum flying weather to get to Arctic Bay and back without refuelling. But the weather didn't cooperate. His flying time was cut in half by a fierce headwind under a heavily overcast sky. Reluctantly, he turned back to Igloolik. After some sleep, he took off again the following morning, this time leaving the mechanic at Igloolik and replacing his weight with four small barrels of gasoline.

The weather was better on this day, at least for the first part of the flight. He knew that following Admiralty Inlet northbound would take him almost to his destination. But about fifty miles out from Arctic Bay the wind became so strong at higher altitudes that Schulte had to descend to only six feet above the water. Just before noon he flew down Adams Sound, banked his plane at Uluksan Point—to the astonishment of the Inuit camped there, who had never seen an airplane before—and landed in front of the trading post at Arctic Bay. The trip had taken four and a half hours.

Close to the post was a small white tent with a cross on top. But Allen Scott had moved the priest into the comfort of his own home and looked after him as best he could. "He is alive but he is in great pain," were Scott's words to the Flying Priest. Cochard wept at the sight of this earthly saviour.

Aboard the plane, Schulte made the patient, dressed in caribou furs and lying on skins, as comfortable as possible. At four o'clock the plane rose through the rain and fog of Arctic Bay. Aided by a tailwind and flying at five thousand feet, the *Flying Cross* reached Igloolik in two and a half hours. After quickly refuelling and picking up his mechanic, Schulte was off again for the most harrowing leg of the journey, through fog at low altitude to Repulse Bay. He landed there in the midnight half-light of a waning summer, with little fuel left. Cochard was taken ashore to rest at Our Lady of the Snows Mission. He spent a sleepless night, racked by fever and pain.

Early in the afternoon of the next day, Schulte landed the *Flying Cross* at Chesterfield Inlet, where there was a resident doctor, Thomas Melling. The Hudson's Bay Company supply ship *Nascopie* was also there, and its physician, Dr. Roger, assisted Melling in his diagnosis. They found a severe kidney infection. The Grey Nuns at the local hospital took charge of Father Cochard and nursed him back to health.

This was the first air rescue to the High Arctic. It was a daring undertaking, in an era of primitive aircraft and before airstrips and navigational aids. Father Paul Schulte received a special paternal blessing from Pope Pius XI for his service.

Operation Canon

John Turner's Tragedy
at Moffet Inlet

J ohn Hudspith Turner was born in England in July 1905, four months after the death of his father. Young John was close to his two brothers and grew into a popular young man, athletic, a swimmer—"a fearless, strapping young man, self-confident but never arrogant ... wholesome but not particularly religious."

In March 1926, John and his brother Arthur both answered the call of the foreign mission field and joined the Bible Churchmen's Missionary Society, an evangelical group formed four years earlier as a reaction against liberal theological views in the Church of England. Both men felt called to work in the Canadian Arctic.

In 1915 the Church Missionary Society had withdrawn from Arctic work, and the mission stations were left in the hands of partially trained native catechists. Ten years later the Bishop of

In Those Days

Moosonee appealed to the new society to reopen this Arctic work. It was this call that the Turner brothers answered.

Arthur Turner left for Pangnirtung in 1928. The next year, John, twenty-four years of age, set out for Pond Inlet. He and fellow missionary Harold Duncan travelled aboard the Hudson's Bay Company ship *Nascopie* to establish the most northerly mission in the British Empire. When they arrived on September 2, the Inuit immediately gave both newcomers Inuktitut names. Turner, although not a short man, was called Mikinirsaq—"the smaller one"—because he was shorter than Harold Duncan—Anginirsaq—who stood well over six feet tall.

The *Nascopie's* crew helped Turner and Duncan erect the framework of their mission house. But with the ship's departure, the rest of the construction was left to the missionaries and the Inuit who helped them. They were not the only missionaries there, however. That same year, two Roman Catholic priests also arrived at Pond Inlet. Only 380 Inuit lived in northern Baffin Island, in widely scattered camps. Most visited Pond Inlet only sporadically to trade at the Hudson's Bay Company post there. Suddenly there were four missionaries vying for their attention.

The representatives of the two competing faiths did not get along with each other anywhere in the Arctic in those days. In fact, for years the Catholic and Anglican clergy at Pond Inlet never even spoke to each other. In 1931 Turner wrote in his diary: "The R. C's. have been more active this year and just recently I felt led to give some direct warning against them ... when I learned of definite attempts by our adversaries to pervert the people— and you are not ignorant of Rome's devices—I felt the time had come for something more aggressive." In Turner's diary for 1946 he wrote: "Those who have been asked here why they follow the priests have acknowledged that they have no desire to do so but simply respond to pressure. The priest tells them that unless they follow him they will die."

Some years earlier he had written in his journal of a church service he had held in a snow house. "This morning just as we started our service in one of the snow houses here I was surprised to see one of the priests coming in." The priest listened to Turner's service, then rose and said he had his own message for the people. There followed a theological argument in the presence of the congregation. A biographer of Turner wrote, "It is a hard thing for primitive Eskimo to see white men, professing to follow the Lord Jesus Christ, who will not shake hands or greet one another."

Because the Inuit population lived in widely dispersed camps, John Turner became a skilled traveller by dog team. From Pond Inlet he travelled to Pangnirtung to visit his brother in 1935. In the winter of 1940–41 he crossed Baffin Island from the Clyde River area to Foxe Basin. His travels took him south as far as Repulse Bay (now Naujaat) and west to King William Island, as well as all over north Baffin. A biographer estimated that in his entire Arctic career, Turner travelled 24,300 miles by dog sled, a distance almost equivalent to travelling around the world.

During his seventeen years of missionary work, Turner returned to England only twice, first in 1933 and again in 1939, each time for one winter.

In the fall of 1937 Turner left Pond Inlet by sled for Arctic Bay, in search of a site for a new mission station. On December 3 he wrote these words in his diary:

"Arrived at Sioralik (Moffet Inlet) feeling definitely that this is God's will to stop and build here. Snow was deep and going hard on dogs for whom we had not much reserve food. Huge

In Those Days

loads—the native had a load of stores and I had lumber for shack (including door, windows, nails—130 pounds) besides 400 or 500 pounds of other gear."

The rest of the construction is treated succinctly: "December 4. Finish foundations and floor of store and begin sides. Temperature −43°F. Cold on hands!" "December 11. Go into store—leaving David (native helper) and family in an 'igloo' (snow house). NOT enough wood to finish store roof so use sail."

For a time the mission at Moffet Inlet—Siuralik in modern Inuktitut orthography—was used only sporadically, during Turner's travels to that area. Eventually it would become his home, and the site of a horrible tragedy.

* * *

In England during the winter of 1939–40, John Turner met a young woman, Joan Hobart. But he returned to the Arctic alone. In 1943 he sent for her, and the following year she travelled to Pond Inlet aboard the *Nascopie*. They were married a few hours after her arrival. The following year a daughter, June, was born. That summer, Turner left the work at Pond Inlet to other missionaries, and the family moved to the isolated two-room house at Moffet Inlet. The next September another daughter, Barbara Grace, was born.

At ship-time in 1947 the Turners were at Arctic Bay to pick up supplies, then returned to Moffet Inlet in their boat, the *Ebenezer*. John was anxious to get back to his translation work. He was at the peak of his productivity. He had revised the New Testament in Inuktitut, prepared a number of books of the Old Testament for publication, translated many hymns, and almost completed the translation of the Book of Common Prayer.

On September 24, two young Inuit girls, Rebecca (who lived with the Turners) and Elizabeth, were outside breaking up ice to carry indoors to replenish the Turners' fresh water supply. One called that there was a seal near the shore. John picked up his rifle and went outside. On his return, he slipped the gun under his left arm so that he could help Elizabeth carry her bucket of ice up the steps. Somehow, the trigger was released. The bullet tore through his upper lip, fractured the base of his skull, and entered the right side of his brain. He fell backwards down the steps and into the snow. Joan, six months pregnant, had been trained as a nurse and administered first aid.

David Tuurngaaluk headed for Arctic Bay in the mission boat to summon help. Ed Jordan, a radio operator there, transmitted a call for help, and John Cormack of the HBC hurried southward in the company's motor launch to assist Joan. The Department of National Defence mounted a rescue operation. But it would be a difficult rescue. There were no airstrips in the area, and the district was virtually unmapped. Graham Rowley, a veteran Arctic explorer with the federal government, and Reverend Maurice Flint, who had been for a time at Moffet Inlet with Turner, participated in the planning. Turner had been promoted to the position of canon in the church in 1939, and so the rescue mission was dubbed "Operation Canon."

On October 2 a heavily laden Dakota aircraft left Winnipeg bound for the Arctic. After stops at Churchill and Southampton Island, the plane made for Moffet Inlet. Joan heard the plane through thick fog in the late morning of October 4. Her husband was in bad shape, his breathing poor. Everything depended on the weather. Then, miraculously, the fog lifted, and the airmen sighted the mission.

In Those Days

Four paratroopers jumped over a frozen lake nearby, and the plane returned to its base. Captain Ross Willoughby, a doctor, administered what care he could to the patient, whose left side was completely paralyzed. The rest of the party scoured the area for a suitable place for the ski-equipped Dakota to land. Finally, in early November, a landing strip was prepared on a lake twenty-three miles south of the mission.

Throughout all this, John Turner remained optimistic. He even interpreted when necessary for his rescuers. On his last Sunday there, he made a futile attempt to play the concertina with one hand, while Inuit prayed with his family in an adjoining room. Finally, on November 21, almost two months after his gunshot wound to the head, it was time for John Turner to leave. Noah Piugaattuk, who had accompanied Turner on so many sled trips in the past, drove him on his last journey to the frozen lake where the plane, named the *Blizzard Belle*, awaited.

Piugaattuk had his own idea of what had caused his friend's accident. It was all the fault of a shaman who resented Turner's attempts to extend the gospel westward to the Nattilingmiut Inuit. Over four decades later Piugaattuk recalled, "His mental condition had changed as well as his way of doing things which resulted in this unfortunate accident. As it turned out this was the work of a shaman from the Nattilingmiut who was able to beat this minister."

After a delay of some hours occasioned by bad weather, the plane took off. It overnighted at Coral Harbour on Southampton Island and reached Winnipeg late the following afternoon.

Canon Turner was immediately taken to the Winnipeg General Hospital, where a medical team gave him the best of care. But his left side remained paralyzed. Although he remained conscious and was able to recognize people and talk a little, his condition was deteriorating. On December 6 he lost consciousness. Three days later he died.

John Turner's wife and two daughters had travelled to Winnipeg aboard the rescue plane, accompanied by the Inuit girl, Rebecca, who had lived with them in Moffet Inlet. His third daughter, Faith, was born to Joan a few weeks after John's death. John Hudspith Turner was laid to rest in the cemetery of St. John's Cathedral, Winnipeg. His family departed soon after for England.

Noah Piugaattuk apparently thought that Turner might have lived if he had remained at Moffet Inlet among the Inuit. He said, "He passed away as a result of a shamanistic curse placed on him. While he was at his home he was recovering slowly as a result of prayers offered to him."

Perhaps one of John Turner's diary entries from earlier in the year of his death should be his epitaph: "I love this country and its people.... This is my first love."

"And the Stars Shall Fall from Heaven"

The Belcher Island Murders

One night in February 1942 a shooting star streaked through the night sky above the Belcher Islands, a remote island group in southern Hudson Bay. Inuit looked heavenward and remembered a Bible verse from Matthew 24: "And the stars shall fall from heaven ... and they shall see the Son of Man coming in the clouds of heaven with power and great glory."

In the winter of 1940–41 Inuit from the southern group of the Belcher Islands had had vigorous discussions on the meaning of various parts of the Bible. Most of them owned copies of the book printed in the Syllabic orthography. They could read the words, but understanding was another matter. No missionary had ever been resident in the islands, and the Inuit had not had the benefit of any religious instruction. Different Inuit put different interpretations on what they read, and interpreted it in light of the comet they had seen. Some came to the conclusion that the end of the world was near.

Shortly thereafter nine Inuit would be dead, victims of religious fervour led by two local men, Peter Sala and Charlie Ouyerack, who had proclaimed themselves to be God and Jesus.

Peter Sala was described as "a natural leader" and "one of the best hunters on the islands." Later reports also described him as being sly and evasive. Ouyerack was described as "a quiet, sickly type of man."

Many Inuit prayed to the two self-proclaimed holy men. The RCMP later reported that "some natives destroyed their rifles and dogs, believing that they would have no further use for them due to the imminent end of the world."

But not all Inuit believed in the teachings of the local prophets. Keytoweiack, a lay reader, who had perhaps studied the Bible more than the others, was one. So was a young man, Alec Ekpuk, and a sixteen-year-old girl named Sarah Apawkok. On January 25, Sarah was forced to attend a prayer meeting in a snow house. When asked if she believed in the teachings of Sala and Ouyerack, she was frightened and said yes. Unfortunately, the others present didn't believe her, and her brother beat her until she fell unconscious. Ouyerack, asked what should happen to her, said that she should die, whereupon five Inuit dragged her outside, and a young woman only a year older then her beat her to death with a rifle. The next to die was Keytoweiack. The prophets had decided that he was Satan and must die. They ordered Adlaykok to kill him. He dutifully fired two shots through the window of an igloo, killing the man instantly.

Ouyerack then moved his camp to Tukaruk Island, where three other families lived. There he ordered Quarack to kill Alec Ekpuk, who happened to be Quarack's son-in-law, because he did not believe that Ouyerack was Jesus. Quarack obeyed the order and killed the man with three shots to his body. The RCMP reported that "the natives all rejoiced that Satan was dead."

The death toll at this time was three. But in early March things escalated when Peter Sala's sister Mina went mad.

An official report recounted:

On March 9th, whilst Quarack was away hunting and Sala was absent on a trip to Great Whale River ... Eskimo female Mina, wife of Moses, suddenly became hysterical or insane, and ran to the various igloos in the camp shouting that Jesus was coming to earth and that they must go out to meet Him. Moses ... and all of the women and children in the camp, with the exception of Quarack's wife, followed Mina out on to the sea ice. Before leaving the shore some of them took off their parkas at Mina's bidding, and Mina and her sister, Kumudluk Sarah, took the parkas off some of the younger children. Mina told them that as Jesus was coming they should meet him in their naked state.

She led the party a long way out on to the ice, walking ahead of them, lifting her hands towards the sky and saying, "Come Jesus, Come Jesus."[1]

[1] Typescript, "Taken from the Annual Report of 'G' Division, R. C. M. Police, Ottawa, for the year ended March 31st, 1942, page 17," as attachment to letter

They came to a stop, and Kumudluk Sarah persuaded the people to take off their remaining clothing and to stay there to meet Jesus. These two women helped to undress some of the children.

In the meantime, Quarack's wife, who had not been influenced by Mina's mad notion, arrived on the scene and rescued one of her children. Her arrival apparently helped to bring the adult natives to a more rational state of mind, but by this time all of the natives including the children were suffering from frostbite and some were in a state of numbness. Quarack's wife persuaded those who could to put on their clothing and she encouraged them to try to clothe and try to save the others who could not help themselves. Mina returned to camp; her husband, Moses, returned carrying a young boy; Minna, wife of Peter Sala, returned carrying her infant.[2]

Two other women returned to camp, each carrying a child. Two women and four children were too numb to move. They remained on the ice and froze to death. The two dead women were Peter Sala and Mina's mother and their sister, Kumudluk Sarah, who was the mother of two of the dead children. The other two were the son and stepson of Peter Sala.

Peter Sala was away when the six deaths on the ice occurred. He had travelled to Great Whale River with the Hudson's Bay

---

from "D. J. Martin, Superintendent, to the Commissioner, R. C. M. Police, 8 March 1944, in RCMP HQ File 41 D 636-13-L-1, copy in author's personal collection.

[2] Ibid.

Company manager Ernie Riddell, who knew nothing of the deaths. While there Peter told an old company pensioner, whom the Inuit regarded as their "white brother," of the murders of the two men and the teenage girl. The pensioner informed Riddell, who radioed the news out to his headquarters and asked that the police be informed. Sala, Riddell, and a missionary immediately set out for the Belcher Islands. "When they returned Sala learned of the death from exposure of his mother and sister and two children and learned to his sorrow that the religious hysteria in which he had taken a leading part was the cause of their deaths."

It was not until April 11 that the police plane arrived with an investigative team.

* * *

The investigation into the Belcher Island murders began on April 13. It was led by RCMP Corporal W. G. Kerr and assisted by Dr. T. J. Orford, with Reverend C. Neilsen acting as interpreter. The bodies of the deceased were examined. Back at the Hudson's Bay Company post, a coroner's inquiry was held. The Inuit did not attempt to conceal any of the tragic details of the deaths.

Dr. Orford served a dual role. He was coroner but also justice of the peace. In the latter capacity he charged Mina with murder for her role in the deaths of the two women and four children. Peter Quarack was charged with murder in the death of Alec Ekpuk. Adlaykok was charged with the murder of Keytoweiack on the basis of information provided by Peter Sala, who was "evasive in regard to his part in the murders." The three Inuit thus far charged were transferred to Moose Factory to await trial. Mina went "violently insane" there and was transferred to a psychiatric hospital in Toronto.

In July a police party travelled to the Belcher Islands to continue their investigation and hold a preliminary hearing. The three accused were brought back from Moose Factory for this purpose. The further investigation and examination of the remaining bodies resulted in murder charges being laid against Peter Sala, Ouyerack, Alec Apawkok, and the young woman, Akeenik. All seven prisoners were committed in custody to await trial.

While awaiting the arrival of the court party, an influenza epidemic struck the islands. At one point forty-six Inuit were down with the flu. One elderly woman died.

The judicial party arrived in the islands on August 18. Judge Plaxton was from the Ontario Supreme Court but was also a stipendiary magistrate for the Northwest Territories. R. A. Olmsted, from the federal Department of Justice, was the prosecutor. J. P. Madden, a lawyer from Ottawa, was defence counsel. Two reporters, one from the Canadian Press and one from the *Toronto Star*, accompanied the party.

The trial began the following day. The jury consisted of six white men: a mining executive, a prospector, the engineer of the HBC vessel *Fort Charles,* the HBC post manager, and, amazingly, both newspaper reporters. The trial proceeded smoothly for six of the accused. But when it was time for Mina's trial, she refused to leave her tent, and "struggled and screamed and sobbed violently. She had to be carried into Court strapped to a stretcher."

In his address to the jury, the judge noted what he called the Inuit's "easy susceptibility to religious frenzy and hysteria particularly when they were left alone without religious guidance or Police supervision, but pointed out that nevertheless the Criminal laws of Canada were just as applicable to these people as they are to their white brethren."

The jury deliberated for a number of hours before bringing in their verdicts. Alec Apawkok was acquitted. The young lady Akeenik was found not guilty on account of temporary insanity. Peter Sala, Ouyerack, Quarack, and Adlaykok were all found guilty of manslaughter, with strong recommendations for mercy in the case of Adlaykok and Quarack, the latter because "he was one of the best hunters on the Islands and had the best fed and best clothed family on the Islands, and was ordinarily a quiet man who usually lived and hunted somewhat apart from the other natives and would probably have remained aloof from the religious hysteria had he not been sought out and influenced by the others." In Mina's case, the defence counsel entered no plea, and the jury brought in a verdict that she was insane.

Peter Sala and Ouyerack were sentenced to two years imprisonment, and Adlaykok to one year, all with hard labour at the RCMP post at Chesterfield Inlet. It was too late in the season for them to be transported to Chesterfield, so they spent the winter at Moose Factory, as did Akeenik and Mina. Quarack was given a two-year suspended sentence and ordered to hunt for, feed, and protect the family of Peter Sala while Sala was imprisoned.

Charlie Ouyerack died at Moose Factory in May 1942. In the summer of that same year the four remaining prisoners were granted early release on the condition that none return to the Belcher Islands. They were transferred by plane from Moose Factory to Great Whale River. The two females were to be transferred to the care of the Reverend Neilsen, from whom they would receive religious instruction. He, however, had no room to accommodate them.

Peter Sala, his family, and his sister Mina moved to the Nasta-poka Islands, north of Richmond Gulf. Mina's husband, Moses, drowned off the coast of the Belcher Islands in the fall of 1943 before he was able to join her. Adlaykok lived in a camp twenty miles north of Great Whale River. Akeenik lived in the same camp. Quarack remained on the Belcher Islands.

In a brief report in 1944, the RCMP noted that the former prisoners had "been living normal lives and the chief instigators, both while serving imprisonment and since being released and returned to their natural environment have conducted them-selves in a normal manner and are now following their normal mode of living."

Peter Sala eventually returned to the Belcher Islands and died there in 1990.

Donald Whitbread
Learning Inuktitut the Old Way

Reverend (later Archdeacon) Donald Whitbread was well known throughout Nunavut and parts of Nunavik. Among other places, he ministered in Frobisher Bay (now Iqaluit), Spence Bay (now Taloyoak), and Broughton Island (now Qikiqtarjuaq). Inuit knew him, and old-timers will remember him, by his Inuktitut name, Quinijuq—the fat one. Looking rather like a cross between Burl Ives and Santa Claus, with rosy cheeks and a long beard, he was an old-style missionary, stern and dogmatic, yet hospitable and extremely kind to those who showed an interest in learning the Inuit language.

I knew him in Broughton Island in 1967 and 1968, after returning there from Padloping Island. I got my real start in language learning with the Inuit who were my teachers in Padloping. Back in Broughton, I sought out Don's assistance in learning some of the fine points and nuances that had eluded me. Not everyone loves the study of grammar, but I do, and so did Don, and so he was an ideal teacher.

Recently I came across a document, lost in my own files for who knows how long, that contained a report presented at the First Synod of the Diocese of the Arctic, held in All Saints Cathedral Hall in Aklavik in 1961. The particular document is one that Don had presented, called "The Necessity For and Methods of Learning the Eskimo Language."

Don suggested that "direct learning from mixing with the people is the only feasible method" for learning Inuktitut. He recommended the following approaches, many of which are as appropriate today as when Don wrote half a century ago:

1. Allow a good concentration, e.g. in camps, out of sight of whites....
2. Make it a major task, not a task to be done along with a lot of others....
3. Set a pattern of learning. Canon Daulby advises five words a day—this is 1,500 words a year....
4. Learn it from the natives themselves, not second hand.
5. Use the words, by learning a little grammar as you go.
6. Listen and get the feel of the language.
7. Remember that most of the hymns and prayers were translated by veterans, and analysis of their translation can show you how the language holds together and what order is found.
8. Always revise your vocabulary every few months for pronunciation.

9. Find someone else to teach it to; you'll learn quickly
    that way.
10. USE it, experiment with hymns, translating prayers, com-
    posing sermons, writing to people, visiting and convers-
    ing, etc. Under all circumstances, force yourself to use it
    and you will learn it.[1]

In the discussion that followed, Don made the observation,
"In the eyes of the Eskimos, ministers are not considered ministers until they learn the language and can speak to the people."

His comment was endorsed by Simonee, who spoke about the
situation at Frobisher Bay: "There is only one white minister at
Frobisher Bay and it is so hard for the minister to learn Eskimo
because of the number of white people." (And this was in 1961!)
He went on, "The minister should go away and get on the trail to
learn Eskimo customs, etc."

In Broughton Island, Don taught a civics course once a week
in the evening in the community hall. This was in the days
before television, and so such a course was well attended. I
often accompanied him on those evenings because it allowed
me to see the language in operation in a formal context, quite
different from the routine of settlement life. I remember that
Don was impressed with my progress in learning Inuktitut. One
night he was speaking to the Inuit about the development of
responsible government in Canada in the 1800s, and when he
came to the part on Lord Durham's report he suddenly handed

---

[1] Don Whitbread, "The Necessity For and Methods of Learning the Eskimo
Language," paper presented at the First Synod of the Diocese of the Arctic
(Aklavik, NT, 1961).

his notes to me, told me that he had to go to the airstrip to meet a plane, and asked me to finish the lesson. I dread to think what the Inuit might have taken away from my humble efforts that evening!

Many people remember Don Whitbread for various reasons. He was a controversial man, both within and outside the church. I remember him as a language teacher, in the tradition of so many of the missionaries who preceded him.

A Well-Travelled Inuktitut Bible

I collect Inuktitut Bibles, among other rare Inuktitut-language items. The older the better. But one of the most treasured items in my collection is not terribly old. It is a copy of *The First Book of Moses Called Genesis*, published in London by the British and Foreign Bible Society in 1934. It is bound in black, with no decoration except two gold-stamped words on the upper right cover, saying *Eskimo Genesis*.

What you know about earlier owners of a book is said to be the book's provenance. And this book has a most interesting history, very personal to me.

I first saw the book many years ago in Toronto, when the well-known Arctic collector George Luste invited me to his home to see his library. I spotted this lovely volume and knew that I had to have it.

Let me describe first what peculiarities of this particular volume interested me. Pasted on the inside front cover is a bookplate with the name William B. Hoyt. Above that, in pen, is the signature Gladys E. McAndrew. On the next page, the front flyleaf, which is otherwise blank, is an inscription in Inuktitut Syllabics, and then an address in Hamilton, Ontario, embossed in raised, uncoloured lettering (which therefore doesn't show up in a photograph). At the foot of that page is the date February 1953. On the reverse of the end flyleaf, at the back of the book, are three lines of Syllabics, followed by a date.

Why did these details excite me?

The writing in Syllabics on the front flyleaf said (transliterated into English letters) *Panigusingmut Mairimut*. We'll forgive the writer his one error—the first word should have been *Panigusirmut*. This means *To Mary Panigusiq*. Young Inuit today would probably only add the directional suffix *–mut* to the last of her two names, but it was common at the time to add it to both. This name meant something to me because Mary Panigusiq was the name, before marriage, of the woman who became Mary Cousins. And she was my mother-in-law.

The inscription had been written by someone who was giving or sending this book to Mary, and the date at the bottom of the page, February 1953, told when.

Now to the three lines of Syllabics on the end flyleaf. They are written by a different hand, with only a few finals. Transliterated into Roman orthography, they read:

Ajuriqsuijimit
Naksiujjusiakka
Kuriapamiiluta

In Those Days

Translated, they mean: "The gift that was sent to me (carried to me) from the minister when we were living at Craig Harbour (Kuriapa)." So Mary wrote this herself.

And when did this happen? The next line tells us: May 13, 1953.

Who was this mysterious minister? The use of the word *ajuriq-suiji* tells us that he was a Protestant minister, not a Catholic. And the dates—February 1953 for the inscription by the missionary, and May 13 of the same year for Mary's receipt of it, or at least the date that she wrote in it—tell us that the book must have been carried in a spring packet of mail by dog sled to Craig Harbour on Ellesmere Island, for the date is far too early for the arrival of a ship. The nearest community with a mission was Pond Inlet, and it happened to be Mary's home community. She knew the minister there, and for three years she had even attended the mission school run there by his wife. So the minister can only have been Reverend Tom Daulby.

Mary was fifteen years old in 1953. She had moved with her father, Lazaroosie Kyak, an RCMP special constable, her mother, Letia, and their family, as well as her uncle Joe Panipakuttuk and his family, to Craig Harbour two years earlier to assist the white police officers who reopened the already twice abandoned police post there. Historically, Canadian Inuit had not lived that far north, and the new places where they lived and travelled in the service of the police had no traditional Inuit names. So Mary's writing in syllabics of *Kuriapa* was simply an Inuktitut transliteration of the English name Craig Harbour. (Say it aloud—it works.)

At ship-time in 1953 Mary left Craig Harbour and moved to Hamilton, Ontario, a move arranged by her father with assistance from his trusted friend, RCMP inspector Henry Larsen. Mary knew Larsen well, having travelled through the Northwest

Passage with him in 1944, at the age of six, aboard the RCMP schooner *St. Roch*. She would spend five years in Hamilton, attending school and visiting the many Inuit who were at the tuberculosis sanatorium. It was in this way that she preserved and even added to her knowledge of Inuktitut.

This takes us back to more information contained in the Inuktitut Bible. Mary lived with the family of Gladys E. McAndrew, whose name is on the inside front cover and whose address—38 Dromore Crescent, Hamilton, Ontario—is embossed on the front free flyleaf. That's the address where Mary lived.

So how did this Bible come to be in the library of George Luste in Toronto? At this, I can only guess. Mary eventually left the McAndrew home. It is unlikely that she gave such a treasured possession to Mrs. McAndrew. Probably she lost it in the house. At some later date Mrs. McAndrew would have found it. Eventually, I assume, she sold it to a book dealer, who sold it on to William B. Hoyt, a well-known Arctic collector who lived not far away, in Buffalo, New York. Hoyt died in 1992, and George Luste eventually bought his collection.

Because the book had meaning for me, I eventually convinced George to sell it to me in 2006. That Christmas I gave it to Mary as a Christmas gift. She was very ill with cancer. Tears filled her eyes as she saw her old Bible again and read her own youthful notation in the back. Four months later, Mary passed away. Shortly before her death, she gave the Bible back to me, to remember her by. It is a cherished part of my book collection to this day.

Acknowledgements

All the stories contained in this volume were originally published in the author's column, Taissumani, in *Nunatsiaq News*. Original titles and publication dates are as follows:

"Sedna, the Woman at the Bottom of the Sea" originally appeared under that title on January 10, 2014.

"Wedding at Hvalsey Church" originally appeared under that title on September 16, 2005.

"The First Thanksgiving in North America" originally appeared under that title on October 12, 2012.

"Greenland Language Pioneers" is a collection of three articles that originally appeared as follows:

"Poul Egede: The First Translations" originally appeared as "Poul Egede and the First Translations into Greenlandic" on February 5, 2010.

"Otto Fabricius: Translator and Scholar" originally appeared in two parts as "Inuit Language Pioneer—Otto Fabricius (1744–1822)," Part 1 on February 12, 2010, and Part 2 on February 19, 2010.

"Samuel Kleinschmidt: Orthographic Pioneer" originally appeared as "Samuel Kleinschmidt, Greenlandic Language Pioneer" on February 26, 2010.

"Mikak and the Moravian Church in Labrador" originally appeared under that title in two parts: Part 1 on November 23, 2018, and Part 2 on November 30, 2018.

"Taboos: Numerous and Irksome Rules of Life" is a collection of three articles that originally appeared as follows:

"Taboos about Pregnancy" originally appeared as "Taboos, Numerous and Irksome Life Rules" on March 2, 2012.

"Taboos about Childbirth" originally appeared under that title on March 9, 2012.

"Taboos after Childbirth" originally appeared in two parts: "Taboos after Childbirth" on July 13, 2012, and "More Taboos after Childbirth" on July 20, 2012.

"Erasmus Augustine Kallihiruq: Inuit Theology Student" originally appeared as "Erasmus Augustine Kallihirua Dies in St. John's" on June 10, 2005.

"The Moravian Mission to Cumberland Sound" originally appeared under that title in three parts: Part 1 on September 18, 2009, Part 2 on September 25, 2009, and Part 3 on October 2, 2009.

"The First Inuktitut Language Conference" originally appeared as "November 24, 1865—First Inuktitut Language Conference" on November 18, 2005.

In Those Days

"Father Gasté's Remarkable Journey" originally appeared under that title on October 10, 2014.

"Simon Gibbons—First Inuit Minister" originally appeared as "Simon Gibbons Born, First Inuit Minister" on June 17, 2005.

"Joseph Lofthouse's Wedding Dilemma" originally appeared under that title on February 10, 2012.

"Taboos about Animals" is a collection of four articles that originally appeared as follows:

"Taboos about Sea Mammal Hunting" originally appeared in two parts as "The Seal and its Many Taboos" on November 23, 2012, and "More Taboos—Seal and Bearded Seal" on November 30, 2012.

"Polar Bear Hunting Taboos" originally appeared under that title on November 16, 2012.

"Caribou Taboos" originally appeared under that title on February 8, 2013.

"Taboos and Beliefs about Earth Eggs" originally appeared as "Earth Eggs" on February 15, 2013.

"Edmund Peck: Missionary to the Inuit" originally appeared under that title in two parts: Part 1 on June 12, 2009, and Part 2 on June 19, 2009.

"The Blacklead Island Mission" is a collection of six articles that originally appeared as follows:

"Preaching in a Sealskin Church" originally appeared in two parts as "Preaching in a Sealskin Church" on October 6, 2006, and "A Sealskin Church Eaten by Dogs" on January 21, 2005.

"Tragedy at Blacklead Island" originally appeared under that title on August 11, 2006.

"The First Baptism" originally appeared as "First Inuk Baptism at Blacklead Island" on May 6, 2005.

"Julian Bilby and Annie Sikuliaq: A Missionary and His Lover" originally appeared under that title in two parts: Part 1 on April 13, 2012, and Part 2 on April 20, 2012.

"E. W. T. Greenshield: The Making of a Missionary" originally appeared as "The Making of a Missionary" on May 5, 2006.

"Inuit Catechists at Blacklead Island" originally appeared under that title in two parts: Part 1 on January 11, 2019, and Part 2 on January 25, 2019.

"Becoming a Shaman" is a collection of five articles that originally appeared as follows:

"Igjugaarjuk Becomes a Shaman" originally appeared under that title in two parts: Part 1 on April 19, 2013, and Part 2 on April 26, 2013. To that is added "Saltwater Shamans," which originally appeared on December 2, 2011.

"Kiinaalik Becomes a Shaman" originally appeared under that title on January 3, 2014.

"Niviatsian Becomes a Shaman" originally appeared under that title on September 21, 2007.

"The Wisdom of Aua" originally appeared in two parts, as "The Wisdom of Aua" on July 11, 2008, and "More Wisdom from Aua" on August 8, 2008.

"Aua Meets the Holy Ghost" originally appeared under that title on September 30, 2011.

"Isaac Stringer, The Bishop Who Ate His Boots" originally appeared under that title on November 9, 2018.

"A Church for Lake Harbour" originally appeared as "Church at Lake Harbour Opens" on December 15, 2006.

In Those Days

"Percy Broughton: The Unknown Missionary" originally appeared under that title in three parts: Part 1 on November 5, 2010, Part 2 on November 12, 2010, and Part 3 on November 19, 2010.

"Father Turquetil: First Roman Catholic Bishop of the Arctic" originally appeared under that title on October 19, 2018.

"Missionary Names in Cumberland Sound" originally appeared as "Missionary Names" on June 26, 2009.

"Rules of Life and Death" originally appeared in two parts, as "Death Customs Among the Inland Paadlermiut" on February 7, 2014, and "Rules of Life Among the Qaernermiut" on April 18, 2014.

"'Coming Up Jesusy'" originally appeared under that title in five parts in 2013: Part 1 on November 15, Part 2 on November 22, Part 3 on November 29, Part 4 on December 6, and Part 5 on December 13.

"The Spread of Syllabics" originally appeared under that title on May 30, 2008.

"Orpingalik: 'All My Being is Song'" originally appeared under that title on May 6, 2011.

"The Power of Magic Words" originally appeared under that title on May 13, 2011.

"Mercy Flight to Arctic Bay" originally appeared under that title on August 4, 2006.

"Operation Canon: John Turner's Tragedy at Moffet Inlet" originally appeared in two parts, as "Canon Turner Establishes Mission at Moffet Inlet" on December 2, 2005, and "Canon Turner Dies in a Winnipeg Hospital" on December 9, 2005.

"'And the Stars Shall Fall from Heaven': The Belcher Island Murders" originally appeared under that title in three parts:

Part 1 on December 5, 2014, Part 2 on December 12, 2014,
and Part 3 on December 19, 2014.

"Donald Whitbread: Learning Inuktitut the Old Way" originally
appeared as "Learning Inuktitut the Old Way" on February 18,
2011.

"A Well-Travelled Inuktitut Bible" originally appeared under that
title on August 17, 2018.

Iqaluit • Toronto